The Secretary's Guide to Church Office Management

ABINGDON PRESS
Nashville

THE SECRETARY'S GUIDE TO CHURCH OFFICE MANAGEMENT

This book is printed on acid-free paper.

Library of Congress Cataloging in Publication Data

Main entry under title:
Secretary's guide to church office management.
1. Church secretaries. 2. Office management.

BV705.S43 1985 254 85-9035

ISBN 0-687-37131-7

MANUFACTURED BY THE PARTHENON PRESS AT
NASHVILLE, TENNESSEE, UNITED STATES OF AMERICA

CONTENTS

CHAPTER 1

SECRETARIES

A secretary is on the front line of a congregation. The office is the focus for a church. How correspondence is handled, phone calls are made and answered, information about the church and its programs is dispensed, and schedules are maintained are critical to the continuing life of a church. These chores are done in the office by a secretary.

This doesn't mean that every church has a clearly defined office or that every congregation has a paid secretary. Small-membership churches often function without a secretary. However, someone, or several someones, in these churches must assume responsibility for keeping track of the life of the church.

The people taking over these roles might be members or a part-time pastor. As a result, the church's office desk might be in the shirt pocket or the purse of a church officer. No matter how informal the procedures used, every church must deal with administrative and planning details. When there is no secretary, volunteers, including the pastor, must make certain that secretarial tasks are cared for.

The secretary is both a position and a person. It is for this reason that a chapter on secretaries is included in this book for secretaries. The tasks ascribed to a secretary are basic to the survival of an office. However, when a secretary begins to work for a church, jobs seem to multiply. As this happens, the potential for abuse and unrealistic expectations mounts dramatically.

Suppose a volunteer agrees to be a secretary with the stipulation that most of the work will be done in her home. She wants to do the work there because she doesn't have to hire a baby sitter or because she can't get around easily. The proposal is accepted by the church. How can such a secretary be abused?

Very simply, abuse takes place when a request exceeds the ground rules agreed to by the volunteer. Most church secretaries are confronted with demands and expectations from church members and the pastor which are beyond the original agreements between the secretary and the church. It makes little difference where the work is done, the fact is that a congregation generates expectations of a secretary as soon as someone assumes secretarial duties.

Suppose the volunteer agrees to do the stencil for the bulletin each week. The agreement with her is that all items to be included in the bulletin are to be given to her by Wednesday. She is supposed to have the stencil ready for duplication on Friday.

This arrangement is publicized throughout the church. It works well for about a month. Then someone forgets and calls on Friday morning demanding that a notice be put into the bulletin. The volunteer can comply by retyping the stencil, or she can refuse. Most often, she will retype the stencil. This is abuse. She has wasted the time it took to type the first stencil.

It makes no difference whether the belated request came as a result of forgetfulness or an emergency. Alternative processes are available for getting the item before the congregation. However, once such an incident occurs, other members will take advantage of the volunteer, and abuse will continue until she changes her own schedule or she resigns. The expectations of her have changed because of this one incident.

Of course, this illustration is as applicable to a paid, full-time secretary as it is to a volunteer. Abuse, in the form of unrealistic demands, is not limited to volunteers. In fact, full-time secretaries must cope with abuse more often than volunteers and with fewer options. Not many full-time secretaries can resign their positions, for example. They are working because they need jobs, in addition to other motivations.

Another kind of abuse is the implied threat. Church secretaries could describe many members as being insensitive. This is a kind description for arrogant. Arrogance is an attitude like, "I'm paying your salary, you'd better do as I say." This can be expressed verbally, and is, to many secretaries, or it can be implied. It is an abusive threat.

Pastors get more demanding as secretaries become more efficient in their roles. Pastors are often afflicted with a procrastination malady. They put off administrative details until the last possible minute. They don't like to write letters, create reports, keep records, or handle financial details even if these are for petty cash. As a consequence, they have to rush to meet imminent deadlines. The person who suffers because of the pastor's poor planning is the secretary. She or he must pull the pastor away from the brink of administrative disaster. This is another form of abuse. It could have been avoided.

Sextons, although essential to church secretaries, are also potential abusers. Even though the sexton is supposed to keep the church clean and to set rooms up for meetings, the secretary hears about it when either or both of these tasks is neglected. For some reason, probably because of proximity, the secretary is criticized for a poorly maintained church and for not having a meeting room ready for a group. "We told you last week we needed the fellowship hall for today's meeting. We even told you how many were coming and how to set up the room. We're here and nothing's done!"

It makes little difference that the secretary passed the message along in writing to the sexton. If the sexton doesn't do the job, the secretary is to blame. That's unwarranted abuse.

Scheduling church use, a task carried jointly by several people and monitored through the church office, is perceived to be the duty of the secretary. In some churches this is a clearly defined job. In most congregations, the secretary has a calendar on the wall on which people write their meetings. Requests for weddings, receptions, or use of the fellowship hall by nonmembers are to be made in writing. This works pretty well, but when there is a foul-up, the secretary is to blame.

For instance, a member of the congregation wants to use the fellowship hall for a wedding reception but gives only the time for the wedding. Another group, seeing the time of the wedding, reserves the fellowship hall for later in the day. The member is very upset because, "The secretary knew I wanted to hold the reception in the fellowship hall." How did the secretary know? The member assumed the secretary should be able to read minds. This is another form of abuse.

In spite of these kinds of abuse, secretaries work for churches. One of their primary motivations for doing so is a sense of mission and ministry. Most church secretaries view their position as more than an office job. They understand it as a means of working with and helping people. They are realistic in their own expectations of how much they can do. Their sense of ministry, while it does not excuse abuse, alleviates the anger and frustration that being abused can cause.

As a means of curtailing some of the more obvious cases of overt abuse of secretaries, an outline of realistic expectations is offered. This outline may not be applicable to every situation, but it contains essentials to be considered by congregations. Even if the secretary is a volunteer, the outline should be studied and adapted to the specifics of the congregation.

Church Secretaries

1. Part-time or Full-time?

The definition of part-time depends on the church. For a small-membership congregation, a one-day-a-week secretary may be full-time. That's all the work the church needs done! To have an individual for more than one day would mean inventing tasks which may be nice but not helpful to the congregation.

A part-time secretary in a church with more than three hundred members could mean anything less than five full work days per week. The work load of a secretary in such a medium-sized congregation may be slight on some days but it would be heavy enough to keep a person around for each day of the week (as the week is defined by the church).

The criterion that distinguishes a full-time from a part-time secretary is the amount of work to be done. If a church needs to have someone answer the telephone for five full work days, that congregation needs a full-time individual (or several part-timers who, together, are the equivalent of a full-time staff person). The status and prestige of a congregation are not legitimate elements in a functional definition of part-time and full-time. A committee of the church which oversees the administrative functions for the congregation must decide whether there is to be a full-time or a part-time secretary.

A congregation may have seasonal needs that dictate having both a full-time and a part-time secretary but at different times of the year. For example, a church in a resort town might, from May through October, triple its membership, attendance at worship, and number of programs. As a result it needs a full-time secretary between April and November (to prepare for and to phase out the season). During December through March, the congregation may need an individual only two days a week.

A secretary can sense the demands of the job and assist the administrative committee to adjust the job to fit the work load. This might be difficult for every secretary, especially one whose livelihood requires a full-time salary. When this is the situation, a careful review of the secretarial demands should be made by the pastor and the administrative committee.

2. *Volunteer or Paid?*

The secretary's position doesn't have to be salaried. Of course, a salaried position gives a committee more control over the individual in it. For instance, an inefficient paid secretary is easier to discipline or replace than is an inefficient volunteer. While neither one may function to the level desired by the church, the degree of control a committee has over a paid incumbent makes discipline easier.

Volunteer secretaries are preferred by some congregations. These churches insist that people express their ministry by doing jobs for the church. One or several persons with secretarial experience are recruited to handle office tasks. In some settings, a group of part-time volunteers schedule themselves into the office so that a full-time work force is managing it. This can happen in congregations with as few as one hundred members.

Creating a position of paid secretary does not mean it will be the only secretarial position in the chuch. Very often, a paid secretary is assisted by several volunteers who do specific tasks. For example, volunteers may come in weekly to type the sermon for duplication, address envelopes for a mailing, or to update mailing and visiting lists. In each instance, the paid secretary lays out the work and helps set the volunteers up with materials and information. In effect, the paid secretary is the supervisor of volunteers.

Some congregations, through the years, move between paid and volunteer secretarial staffs. The reasons for this shift are changing work loads and the number of volunteers available. Work loads change because different pastors have differing emphases. The number of volunteers mean those who have secretarial experience and interest.

Another reason for changing is when a church decides to rotate between paid and volunteer staff every few years. This decision reflects a plan of ministry and is not entered into haphazardly. A prerequisite for such rotation is a well-organized office with standardized procedures and a competent committee which oversees it.

The decision to use volunteer or paid staff is based on the style of the congregation, not its size. Large congregations function effectively by depending on volunteer office assistance. However, the most frequent arrangement is for at least one paid secretary (either full or part time) and several volunteers who give between one and five hours a week to help in the office. Occasionally, this combination is augmented for special needs by additional volunteers or temporaries (including high school students).

3. *Hours and Overtime*

A church office has two main functions: (1) to maintain the church by performing administrative activities and (2) to serve the congregation. Setting office hours to handle administrative details does not serve many congregations adequately.

One of the principal culprits in establishing office hours for administrative purposes only is the pastor. Pastors often think the office exists only to assist them. The pastor needs help in understanding that the church office is not for her or his personal convenience but is there to serve church members. If the office doesn't serve the congregation, the church's volunteer corps will dwindle to those who can work within the established hours. This seriously limits the program possibilities of the congregation.

A church which insists on having its office open between 9:00 A.M. and 5:00 P.M. or 8:00 A.M. and 4:00 P.M. on Monday through Friday cannot be interested in serving its people. Members who hold jobs are tied up during these hours unless they work swing shifts. Executives and managerial people can call during the day, but few service and factory people want to use their break time to call the church. No matter when they can call, if members who work want or need to get something from or take something in to the office they must make special arrangements with the sexton or the pastor.

A church with a competent secretary doesn't need the pastor there whenever the office is open. Therefore, adjusting the schedule to the pastor's preferences is not in the best interests of the church. The secretary can handle most items coming into the office such as giving out routine information, providing directions to hospitals or nursing homes, updating people on who is in the hospital and convalescing, giving out schedules for meetings, noting requests fo materials, ordering and receiving items, and listening to and recording complaints. The pastor doesn't need to be present all the time to oversee a competent secretary.

In considering alternative schedules, having the office open on Saturdays, at least until about 1:00 P.M., would be very helpful in many communities. In other settings, having daily office hours from 1:00 P.M. until 6:30 P.M. would be beneficial. In certain situations, daily office hours might be from 9:00 A.M. until 12:00 noon and from 7:00 P.M. until 9:00 P.M. Scheduling office hours should allow an office to do both the administrative and the congregational service functions well. To neglect either is to weaken the ministry of the church.

Posting office hours tells the community which of its people the church is interested in serving. A church decides who it is going to serve not only by its evangelism program but by its office hours as well. A church secretary knows which groups in the community the church is serving because she or he knows who can and who can't be served by the office during its posted hours. With some assistance from their secretaries, many churches could become attuned to a wider constituency.

If flexible hours are adopted by an office, what constitutes overtime? Overtime means that an individual works longer than the number of hours he or she was scheduled to work. For instance, if the normal work week is 35 hours and a person puts in those hours by splitting a day and evening shift and working on Saturday, there is no overtime involved. However, if the individual works 37 hours, overtime must be paid for 2 hours beyond the normal 35.

Strict accounting of hours and overtime is essential not only for paid personnel but for volunteers as well. A volunteer's time is as valuable to the church as is the time of a paid secretary. Keeping track of hours worked is not done carefully in most church offices. As a result, the secretary decides how many hours are enough, or a volunteer begins to feel abused. Either of these situations is injurious to the church and to the secretaries.

A few churches have discovered it is easier to hire secretaries for evenings and Saturdays by using incentive pay. This adds a factor of 25 percent (or some other percentage) to the hourly rate paid. Other congregations pay a set rate but hire an individual just to be present in the office without doing any secretarial work.

When the church seeks volunteers for evenings and Saturday office work, an added incentive may be a paid baby sitter or transportation or some other thing that is desirable to the person. People are willing to give an evening or a Saturday morning to the church if there is a need and it entails constructive work. Few want to "office-sit" in a church.

In churches that experiment with office hours, a combination of volunteer and paid secretarial staff works well. Volunteers may take the morning shift, and a paid secretary may handle a late afternoon or evening shift. Saturdays may be split between volunteers and a paid secretary, with each being in the office two Saturdays a month.

4. Vacation and Special Leaves

People who work need time off. They need a change of pace. This may be a vacation scheduled once a year or a shortened work week for several months (the off days accumulating to a specified amount of time) or a few days leave taken here and a few days there. The amount of time off for which a paid individual will continue to receive a salary should be designated in the employment agreement.

Volunteers need time off as well. They need to design, with the person in charge of the office, a schedule for their time out of the office. This will allow the person in charge to find replacements or to hire a temporary employee.

Special leaves, usually called leaves of absence, are sometimes necessary, due to unexpected circumstances. Accidents, births, deaths, and severe disease in a family might cause a volunteer or an employee of the office to ask for a special leave. Such a leave generally is without compensation but carries with it an understanding that the job will be available when he or she can return.

Leaves of absence are granted by the committee overseeing the office. Any person hired or recruited to do the job during the leave must be told that the position is temporary, pending the return of the individual he or she replaced.

Recruiting Church Office Help

A church must be clear about what it wants before it begins recruiting people to do a job. This means a committee overseeing a church office must write job descriptions and expectations. As it does this, the committee has to be aware of the personality and work style of the pastor, since the pastor's influence will be significant.

For instance, if the pastor has trouble delegating responsibility to a secretary, the committee had better not recruit a take-charge person. The resultant clash between the secretary and the pastor will involve more than just the committee!

On the other hand, if the pastor's style is to overlook administrative responsibilities, the church needs a person in the office who keeps track of details. This kind of individual would pick up the pieces of administration and allow the pastor to do other things. However, the secretary should be guided by the administrative committee. No secretary should feel comfortable doing the administrative work of a church without direct accountability.

The committee, as it recruits a secretary, must be aware of how soon a pastor's tenure might end. If the pastor is leaving within a few months, it is well to find a strong, organized secretary. This kind of person will be needed during a transition period, especially if there are to be several months without a pastor. At the same time, the secretary will need to understand that a new pastor will be coming and the work style of the office might change significantly.

Recruiting volunteers for work in the office is different from recruiting a paid secretary. The secretary is assigned to a variety of duties including general supervision of the office. Volunteers should be recruited for specific tasks.

For example, a volunteer may be recruited to type a newsletter stencil. If this task doesn't have typing speed requirements, people who type slowly could be recruited since the primary needs are reliability and accuracy. If the office needs someone to stuff envelopes for a large mailing, several persons who enjoy one another's company might volunteer as a group. Recruiting volunteers for general office work is not a good idea unless there is a volunteer coordinator for the office.

Each job in the church office needs to be covered by a written job description. The description doesn't need to be long and detailed, but it must be accurate. It should identify the qualifications needed, the type of work to be done, and the person to whom the job holder is responsible.

Job descriptions are needed for tasks done by volunteers as well as those done by employees. Job descriptions should be updated regularly, at least every three years, and especially when new machines, procedures, or pastors become part of the office.

Training

Every office worker deserves the courtesy of being trained. Training is a process that helps a person become acquainted with office procedures and policies as well as get comfortable in doing the task for which he or she was recruited. Training may be a few hours of show and tell on the first day of work or it may be an orientation session of an hour or two followed by several days of on-the-job training. No matter how long the initial training session is, in most offices an employee is considered to be on probation for at least three months, during which time continuous training occurs.

Training includes: (1) a review of the job description, (2) a discussion of how one is to keep records, (3) demonstrations on the use of the various office machines, (4) ordering and inventorying supplies, (5) what and where to store office records and materials, and (6) the filing system. In addition to these specifics, training will orient new persons into the work style of the office. A discussion of the office procedures and practices will be a normal part of the ongoing training process.

1. Review of Job Description

Individuals recruited to work in a church office will have seen the description of the tasks for which they have been hired or for which they have volunteered. A review of this description during training should deal with: (1) the types of tasks to be done, (2) the authority limits of each position, (3) the kinds of accountabilities in the office, (4) the regular deadlines imposed by the job, and (5) the normal evaluation procedures used in the office.

Of particular importance is the discussion of the authority limits of a job. For instance, a job might include supervision of others, taking care of a petty cash fund, ordering supplies, and incurring bills of less than a certain figure. In addition, a secretary in charge of an office might be given authority to hire temporaries when the work load gets too heavy. (In some settings, the authority might be to recruit volunteers rather than hire people.) The limits of authority for each job need to be spelled out.

Accountabilities and deadlines should be carefully explained during training. These explanations should be written so that future reference is easy when any questions arise. These written materials, including deadlines; work hours; procedures for taking sick leave, vacation, and special leaves; and grievance processes, should be part of a packet each person receives during training. This might seem to be too formal for small-membership churches, but a page or two outlining expectations can save much time over the long haul. At least one page should be devoted to accountabilities and deadlines.

Evaluation in many church offices is informal; it is done by the pastor or a committee once in a while. Evaluation can be a helpful device for improving a secretary's work style when it is done regularly and in a supportive manner. While evaluation involves criticism, the way it is handled can make a world of difference to those doing the evaluation and those being evaluated.

For example, if evaluation focuses on the ministry of the office it is possible to cite image (accurate typing, good telephone manners, promptness), personal concern (dealing with the public, taking messages, giving information), and action (getting through to the pastor, getting notices out, doing correspondence) as basic elements. Specifics under each of these headings can become topics for evaluative discussion. The evaluator should emphasize improving each of these rather than giving an entirely negative appraisal. In addition, strengths can be noted in each area so the individual, rather than becoming totally discouraged, is given goals to work toward.

Evaluation extends to volunteers in the office. They are as much a part of the church's ministry as is an employee. It is important for them to understand their role in the ministry of the church. It must be understood that volunteers can be asked to find another form of contribution to the church's life when their performance in the church office is detrimental to the office and to the church.

Training should spell out the evaluation process and the fact that a number of poor evaluations will result in being replaced. It should be noted that individuals can be replaced because of their incompetence or because of their attitude. This should occur only after they have been given sufficient opportunity to improve their skills and attitude.

2. *Keeping Records*

The more obvious types of records a secretary keeps are telephone calls, petty cash, and personal items such as hours and days worked. In addition, mailing list corrections; membership records; lists of hospitalizations, of individuals living in nursing homes, and of invalids; and records of similar items that have to do with the ongoing lives of church members are often kept by secretaries. It is essential that these records be accurate and current.

In some churches, secretaries are asked to maintain a visitor's file. This is a list of members, prospective members, and constituency on which is noted each visit by the pastor or by another person representing the church. This list would include a notation that a member was visited as part of the every-member canvass or during a special program of the evangelism committee. Usually these records list the date and time of the visit. Any other notations are considered confidential and should not be part of the public file.

The training session should specify the kinds of records a secretary is expected to keep for the church. A secretary is not required to keep records of a personal nature for the pastor.

3. *Use of Office Machines*

A few churches don't train new office workers to use the office machines until the time comes that they have to use one. For instance, they don't show people how to use a duplicating machine until they have to do some duplicating. This is not a sound practice because it is awkward to try to train someone in the use of a machine when a deadline is near and the work area is crowded. It is best to do the demonstrations during a pre-set training period. It is best, as well, to demonstrate all the machines the individuals are expected to use.

Training should not assume any familiarity with any office machine, no matter how experienced a person may be. Machines change with every model and an individual may know how to run one type but not another. Demonstrate each machine for every new person in the office.

Additional training is needed when new machines are added to an office. If the machine is a computer, a three-month period for becoming acquainted with it will be minimal.

4. *Supplies*

Budgets are limited in every church. That's one reason training should include procedures for inventorying and ordering supplies. A secretary who keeps careful inventories knows when to expect heavy demands on particular kinds of supplies such as paper and envelopes. The secretary will be aware of sales and discounts offered by various office-supply vendors. Ordering supplies during sales will ensure adequate reserves and can alleviate budget strain in most churches.

Training should demonstrate the procedure for keeping a moving inventory. This procedure involves recording each item that has been used and how many like items remain in stock. For instance, when a stencil is used a notation of how many stencils were used is inserted in a "used" column and a new figure is placed in the "stock" column. This notation might look like this:

Stencils: Date: 10/5 Beginning Stock: 24 Used: 2
Date: 10/5 New Stock: 22

A running inventory of each kind of office supply should be kept by the secretary. This account can be updated by having a simple form (like the above) in the room where supplies are kept. Each person who uses supplies should be instructed to make an entry whenever he or she uses any kind of supply. The secretary (or whoever assumes the task of inventory and ordering) would collect these tally sheets on a weekly or monthly basis. Marking the tallied items on a master list would indicate the number of each item that has been used and how many are still in stock. Without such a system, supplies are likely to run short during a time when the budget is too low to order more or when a peak need occurs.

5. *Storage*

The decision-making process for determining what gets stored and where it will be kept should be explained during training. (A discussion of storage of office files and historical documents is contained in chapter 3.) It is most unfortunate to have a valuable file or document discarded because an office worker did not know its value and couldn't decide whom to turn to for a decision on keeping and storing it.

6. *Filing*

The process of filing should be discussed in detail during training (see chapter 3). This part of the training program will involve making decisions about specific types of files. (An exercise using file folders with various labels is a good way to acquaint new office workers with an existing filing system.)

The training time given to filing can assist secretaries to make certain that instructions for filing are in evidence and are clear. (One copy of the instructions for what goes into a file cabinet should be on its outside.) Also, new people should know where to find the key to the file system.

These six points are key elements in a training program. Taking the time when a person is new to acquaint her or him with the office will save much lost motion in the first few weeks and months. Of course, a training process is never complete. People always have questions, and issues arise that have not been anticipated. The last few minutes of the training program should be devoted to listing names of people who can help make decisions on unexpected issues. These people will include the pastor and the chairperson of the committee overseeing the office.

CHAPTER 2

STANDARDIZING PROCEDURES

Two church secretaries met in a restaurant one afternoon for a break. They began comparing notes on their work and working conditions. One said, "It's easy for you to talk about having everything in order, with that person doing this and the other doing that. Your church is so much larger than ours. You have more people working."

"I grant you the size. But that's not the reason things run smoothly. I've made it my business to organize the office and everything in it so people can come in, work, and leave without bothering anyone else."

"How can you manage that?"

"Early in my career I discovered that if I was going to get my work done, there had to be a way to organize things so no one would bother me. My solution was to develop standardized procedures."

"Standardized procedures?"

"Yes. I divided my responsibilities into types and then wrote out policies, instructions for getting the work done, and developed what I call general practices. As time went by, I updated these things. When people asked how to do something or where a particular item was stored or anything like that, I referred them to a folder on my desk. In it they found most of the answers to their questions. That way, I kept on working and they got what they needed."

"That sounds easy. Maybe it's worth a try."

"It isn't easy, especially when you're setting it up. It takes time and a lot of thinking. But once it's done, you begin saving time and frustration. In our church, volunteers can come in without me there and use those folders, do their jobs, and leave without messing up the office or creating hours of additional work for me. I'd recommend it, but don't think it'll be easy to set up."

A church office is a very public work situation. It is not the domain of a secretary. It is a place where a large number of church members come each year for information, to work, and to get access to the building, machines, or supplies. The office is the administrative heart of the church. The secretary's task is to make certain this hub of activity is organized and functions well.

A church secretary quickly learns that being personally organized is important. Much more important to the church is for the secretary to organize an office that stays organized even without her or his presence. As the secretary said, "It's not easy." Creating an office which organizes those who use it is much different from being personally organized. Imposing procedures on people so they will not feel stifled or stymied is the name of your game. Treating people equally without appearing to be impersonal is a test of the organization a secretary establishes.

Nothing is foolproof. However, formulating some procedures that apply to everyone and everything in the office lessens the possibility of frustration and hurt feelings. Other people use the office, its equipment and supplies. They do not want a free hand; neither do they need unwieldly constraints. They must accomplish assignments and must have access to the office. Standardizing office procedures helps them and the secretary.

Getting Started with Standards

Surprisingly, the smaller the office staff, the more critical is the need for office guidelines. In many church offices, the primary task of the secretary, often part-time, is to straighten up after others have done their work. The secretary can't seem to get to many jobs because she or he must spend so much time as a maintenance person.

Churches with a full-time secretary need standards because of the number of volunteers and temporary employees who come and go weekly.

Three types of guidelines are necessary for church offices. These are instructions, policies, and general practices.

1. *Instructions*

Instructions are specific to things or procedures. The primary requirement for instructions is that they be complete enough for a stranger in the office to find what he or she is looking for. Of course, instructions for using everything will not be left on the desk. For instance, the working of the security system should be known by very few individuals. These instructions should be kept in a locked place. But they should be available because people are replaced and the new individuals must know how to get into the building or room without setting off the alarm.

Sometimes instruction sheets are long and detailed, and at other times they are short. Some may have illustrations and some may not. A few might be on microfiche or on computer disk, but even these should have printed directions as backups and a directory telling where they are kept.

Instruction sheets must be kept in an easily accessible place and ought to be clearly marked. Not all of them will need to be on a secretary's desk. Some might be pasted to the outside of a file cabinet, others might be attached to a machine, and others might be posted on a door or wall. A copy of each set of instructions would be in a file over which the secretary has control. One set would be on the secretary's desk.

There are three types of instructions: "how-to," "where-to," and "when-to." The titles are self-explanatory.

A "how-to" instruction tells how something functions, gives directions, or lists procedures to follow. These are the most common type of instructions. They tell people how to get keys, run machines, order supplies, find items in files, look up phone numbers and addresses, and give directions for getting to hospitals, denominational offices, bookstores, printers, and other places important in the life of the congregation.

Another form of instructions is "where-to." These relate to getting approvals, finding and returning items (such as kitchen utensils, church school resources, supplies, and machines), and submitting reports. They might include a changing list of hospitalized persons and people in nursing homes. When this list is posted, much time is saved by secretaries both in looking up the name and in giving directions to the hospital or home.

A third form of instructions is "when-to." These are critical for volunteers assisting with mailings, financial matters (deposits, bank statements, and reports), publicity (getting items in for bulletins, newspapers, and newsletters), and committees or groups (for meeting dates, duplication of minutes, and annual report dates).

When instructions are written out and duplicated, questions can be answered by pointing to a paper or by giving an individual a copy. This saves much time and prevents many interruptions. Developing the instructions takes time, but measured over a year or two, the effort is an investment with long-term dividends.

2. *Policies*

A policy is "a definite course of action adopted for the sake of expediency" *(The Random House College Dictionary*, rev. ed., 1975). The key word is "adopted." A policy, to have authority behind it, is enacted by an official body of the church because this body believes it will assist the church in handling program or administrative matters. Policies relating to the church generally affect the uses of facilities and equipment, and reimbursement for expenses.

A secretary may encourage the creation of a policy based on experience with church members. If this happens, it is important to have the policy approved by an official body of the congregation and the action recorded in that body's minutes. This may seem legalistic, but experiences in congregations indicate that such a process safeguards not only secretaries and clergy but volunteers and others who do business with or work for a church.

A policy is only as good as its observance. Exceptions to any rule negate the effectiveness of the guideline. This is not to call for rigid adherence to every rule or policy. People have needs and emergencies that make policies obstructive. Nevertheless, a secretary must be cautious in making exceptions to policy because those exceptions have a way of becoming precedents for getting around policies.

As with instructions, policies need to be written and posted. This saves many explanations and arguments. A copy should be on file. References to the original action, giving the date, should be included with the policy.

3. General Practices

These are guidelines that deal with the operating style of the office. They have to do with cleanliness, letting the secretary know when something doesn't work, noting that supplies are low, and what to do when one runs into a difficulty and no one is in the office. General practices are more than helpful hints (these should be appended to the instructions). Practices are exactly what they say: "This is the way things are done here."

It isn't necessary or even a good idea to have an excessive number of general practices. However, a volunteer would be helped by knowing the secretary's expectations. A list of these practices can alleviate many difficulties before they become problems.

Review and Update

Instructions, policies, and practices need to be reviewed and revised regularly. For instance, instructions for operating a machine are specific to one kind of machine. If the machine is replaced, new instructions are needed. The need for change occurs when there are any adjustments in the life pattern of a congregation.

Annual reviews of instructions, policies, and general practices will catch a secretary up with change. Many times, a new practice or procedure has evolved and appropriate inserts in instructions have not been made. An annual review will point out this deficiency. In some instances volunteers or temporary workers suggest changes to the secretary. When this happens, thank them and consider their proposals.

If a policy needs changing, the change must proceed

through proper church channels. Usually this requires a written explanation of the change and a vote by the governing body. While the revision may not cause much discussion, it is very important to have it approved by the official body of the church.

Five Areas Needing Policies and General Practices

Instructions are written as each specific need is noted. Among these are ordering procedures, how to use the filing system, and the techniques for operating a machine. There will be a large number of instructions because they are specific to a task.

Policies and general office practices outline procedures to be followed in the office. Consequently, there will be fewer policies than there are sets of instructions. Five types of situations, due to their importance and the possibility of misunderstanding among the many people who use a church office, ought to be covered by policies or handled by clearly outlined office practices. These five are: minutes of meetings, meeting notices, duplication, office equipment use, and use of the telephone.

1. Minutes of Meetings

Minutes, the historical and legal record of a church, can cause many problems. A policy, or at least a general practice, should be formulated to deal with minutes of meetings.

The reason for this need is apparent when a secretary is confronted with questions like: Where are minutes of meetings kept? Which minutes need to be kept? Who is responsible for filing them? Who duplicates them? How are they distributed? Which are legally important? How long should they be kept?

A general assumption is that a secretary will at least duplicate the minutes of each meeting of the most important committees of the church. This assumption may not be accurate. A few committees will not want the secretary to see the discussions and decisions of their meetings. One such committee may be the personnel committee. However, in most congregations this assumption prevails regardless of the normal work load of the secretary. As a result, committee chairpersons get upset when a secretary says she or he has too much other work to do and can't get to the minutes by a certain deadline. Conflict ensues.

A secretary believes church office files should be maintained in a certain manner. This secretary also feels that individuals who need materials from the files should request what they want rather than mess up the files by looking for something themselves. Yet, some congregational leaders file their committee's materials themselves. This tends to create confusion and anger in the office.

Another issue surrounding minutes is the space used for them. Some chairpersons want to keep several copies of the minutes of each meeting in the files. Before long, the files are bulging with duplicate copies of minutes. A policy or general practice should regulate the number of sets of minutes to be kept in the file cabinet and designate a place where additional copies may be stored.

Historical and current files are maintained by some churches in order to accommodate the accumulation of minutes over time. In most of these churches a policy is in force which limits the kinds of meeting minutes included in the historical file. Not every committee's minutes are kept.

The decision regarding which are not retained is covered by a policy or accepted practice in the church office.

A policy regarding minutes should be created jointly by the pastor and secretary and approved by an administrative committee of the church. The policy, to be effectively administered, must be understood by each chairperson of every church committee. Additional copies of the policy will need to be given to individuals who assume leadership roles during a year or who are asked to serve in a short-term capacity. A copy of this policy should be sent annually to committee chairpersons whether they are incoming or incumbents. It never hurts to remind people of a policy.

2. *Notifying People About Meetings*

Volunteers need to be reminded about meetings they should attend. How this is done varies according to church practice and custom. In some churches, members of committees dealing with sensitive issues are reminded of their meetings by a phone call from the chairperson. In other instances, post cards are used to remind members of meetings. In some churches, reminders are not sent because people are expected to remember meetings.

The critical element in reminding people of a meeting is knowing who is a member of a committee and where they live. The chairpersons of most committees in a church think it is the secretary's job to keep the mailing list (with phone numbers) of each church committee. Not only should this list be up to date but the secretary ought to know the meeting schedule. These chairpersons expect the secretary to get a notice to committee members well in advance.

Secretaries, on the other hand, need cooperation from committee chairpersons who must share responsibility for maintaining correct mailing lists and verifying meeting times and places. Often lack of cooperation and communication between committee chairpersons and secretaries creates unnecessary dilemmas.

In most such dilemmas, the secretary becomes the eye of a storm because reminders aren't sent. Yet, who is at fault? Who should decide such issues as: Are the minutes of a previous meeting to be sent? Is the secretary supposed to send a notice for the next meeting? Should this be done for every committee? Who determines which ones don't need reminders? The secretary is not all-knowing. She or he can make decisions, but by which guidelines?

As with minutes of meetings, the secretary and pastor need to formulate a policy or a general practice for reminding people about meetings. This practice would involve creating a list of the committees for which the secretary assumes responsibility for sending out meeting notices. The chairpersons of these committees would be required to check their mailing lists regularly to update names and addresses. The list should state what type of notice is to be sent and for which meetings.

When a question arises about a particular meeting or committee, the pastor and secretary would resolve the issue jointly. If the pastor is not available, the secretary would decide, based on the policy or practice.

3. *Duplicating*

Duplicating is a job many secretaries are willing to give up. It can be messy, it can be frustrating, it is boring, and it uses time that could be more gainfully utilized. Nevertheless, churches depend on the secretary to duplicate bulletins, newsletters, notices of meetings, and minutes of meetings.

The issue here is not whether duplicating is to be done but who is to be in charge of it. An example of this problem is a situation that developed in a city church with a part-time secretary. A volunteer offered to take care of their duplicating jobs, and the congregation accepted the offer. Very soon they realized their error. He put the duplicator in a room for which only he had a key. He kept track of and ordered supplies. He determined the number of copies for each item duplicated.

Needless to say, this set-up became a burden on the congregation within a year. The need for better control of the duplicating function by the secretary was voiced by the secretary, pastor, and congregation. After a confrontation, a new office practice was instituted, which was to have the duplication handled solely by the church secretary.

This illustration points out how sensitive an issue duplicating for the church can become. It involves deadlines, deciding how many copies to make, keeping track of supplies, and determining what is to be copied. These decisions have an impact on the life of the church and should be made by one individual who is accountable to the pastor and to the congregation. Duplicating is a critical process in a congregation. A general practice of the church office should be to aim at doing it efficiently.

It may be necessary to write out rules regarding this practice. However, it is one of those activities which can be regulated rather easily by a secretary so long as she or he is organized.

4. *Using Office Equipment*

Many churches have developed policies regarding the use of, maintenance of, and storage of their office equipment.

They follow these policies rigidly because of the expense of repairs or replacement of any piece of equipment.

As a matter of information, office equipment includes tape recorders, video cassettes, televisions, microphones, dictating equipment, computers, typewriters, and other such items. Usually a church administrative committee or the trustees have established a policy covering all equipment, but sometimes audiovisual equipment is treated differently because it is most often used in the church school. Sometimes the existing policy allows church members access to the equipment at the church for short periods of time or for specific tasks. The separate policies that may govern church-school equipment may put the secretary in a difficult spot.

An office is more efficient when it is well equipped and its equipment is in good condition. However, it runs smoothly only when the equipment and supplies are available and the equipment functions when needed. Therefore, it is mandatory for a secretary to stress to the pastor and administrative committee that they need an enforceable policy regarding office equipment. The policy should state that no equipment should be allowed out of the office. It especially should prohibit the removal of any piece of office equipment from the building.

As a part of the policy, maintenance agreements should be purchased for each piece of equipment so that if it is somehow abused, it can be serviced inexpensively and quickly. The secretary is responsible for keeping office equipment up to par and available when needed. Therefore the secretary should work hard to get policies enacted for use of all equipment, including audiovisual and church-school equipment. If such policies exist, the secretary must have the authority to enforce them.

5. *Telephone*

The office telephone is a communication device for the church and is not there as a convenience for church members. Strict rules need to be set regarding its use.

A policy for telephone use is difficult to make and hard to enforce. This policy must include guidelines for volunteer workers who make calls as part of their duties. However, they must not abuse their tasks by tying up the telephone at busy times of the day nor for long conversations. The policy might designate periods for certain kinds of calls. The policy ought to stipulate that the telephone may be used by choir members who need to contact someone for a ride home after practice. The policy should also provide that the telephone be available for youths to get in touch with parents or guardians after a trip or after a meeting for rides or to get approval for an activity. The telephone must be available to anyone who happens to be in the church and has an emergency, regardless of the hour or day. In some congregations, small containers are put beside the telephone so members can pay for any of these types of calls they have to make.

Often, churches install a pay telephone near a front hall or adjacent to the fellowship area. This coin-operated telephone is in addition to the regular office telephone. It must be kept in good working condition in order to serve its purpose.

In many churches, the office telephone has an extension in a kitchen or a church-school office for which a janitor or the secretary has a key. It is available only when one or the other of them is at the church.

The telephone use policy, in addition to spelling out restrictions, should deal with taking messages. People who may be in the office when the secretary or pastor are out must be taught how to take messages. A small pad placed near each telephone can encourage people to jot down notes and numbers. However, a secretary should not assume that everyone knows how to answer a phone or that he or she will be aware of each call's importance. The secretary must do some training, especially of the custodian.

The secretary should check for messages daily, since calls come in to the church from persons who do not know the minister and at times when the office is closed or is managed by a volunteer. Each call is important.

These five items just discussed need attention from the administrative committee overseeing the work of the church office. In some cases, policies have to be established, and in others the committee may request that the secretary establish a general practice that can be communicated to others who use the office. When the committee sets a policy or asks a secretary to establish a general practice, it must give the secretary enough authority to enforce the policy or practice.

The church secretary must remember, when enforcing policies and creating practices, that others are going to use the office. The place and position are not her or his domain exclusively. Setting solid ground rules should help the secretary and others understand one another and respect the church office as a common, functional part of their ministry.

Office Help

Every church office, at one time or another, has to hire help. The need may occur seasonally, when an unusual amount of work has to be done in a short time. Or it may happen when the regular secretary (paid or volunteer) gets sick or asks for time off. A more serious occasion is when a secretary quits and a replacement must be found. In each of these situations, new people must assume jobs in a church environment. No matter how experienced the people are, adjusting to the demands of this particular church will take time.

In order to relieve as much frustration and lost motion as possible, each congregation should anticipate the need for additional people before they are called. This anticipation should encourage the development of job descriptions, office rules, and evaluation procedures.

1. *Job Descriptions*

A job description should state the qualifications needed for a job (education and experience) as well as identify the types of work that must be done. One section of the description includes special stipulations such as knowing the workings of a church, equal opportunity statements, and working conditions. Such descriptions are necessary for each employee of the church.

The job description for secretaries (part-time, full-time, paid, or volunteer) should identify their normal duties, their accountabilities, and the expectations of the supervising committee of the church. A job description ought to be in place before a secretary is sought and especially before one is hired. A job description gives both the church and the secretary a solid footing on which to build a good working relationship.

2. *Office Rules*

The secretary, the pastor, and the administrative committee of a church should work out office rules. Rules apply to paid employees more than to volunteers. However, some rules relate to office situations and apply equally to paid and volunteer workers.

Office rules define the number of excused absences that can be accepted, the time for opening and closing the office, the length of a secretary's working day; identify who has authority to order supplies and equipment; state who is in charge of the petty cash fund; and list whom to contact for emergency authorization for repairs. Office rules are established to ensure impartial treatment for all employees. Rules can help maintain an organized and effective office.

After guidelines have been created for the regular secretary, the committee should formulate additional rules for people who use the office. These guidelines should cover part-time workers, authority for access to the office after hours, the circumstances under which it is appropriate to do work at home, medical benefits, insurance, and taking supplies and office equipment home to do work. No one should be asked to work who doesn't know the rules of the office.

3. *Evaluation*

Evaluation of office help is very important. The form it takes should be worked out by the administrative committee of the congregation. The evaluative process must include an opportunity for the office workers to discuss the evaluation in a non-threatening context. Evaluation, to be effective, should be done in an impartial manner. Forms can be developed which can be used for regular and special office help.

Evaluations ought to be regularly scheduled events. They can be done by the pastor alone or by the pastor along with members of an administrative committee. The evaluators should be aware of the pressures and demands of the office before they attempt an evaluation.

When There Is No Pastor

A church can lose its pastor and continue to function well as long as its secretary maintains administrative order. The value of a good secretary is often overlooked by a congregation.

In many ways, a secretary is the administrative pastor of a church even when the pastor is present. However, when the pastor is gone, when the pastor is ill, or when there is a change of pastors, the secretary becomes the visible administrator of the church. She or he must handle the telephone calls, make certain correspondence is directed to the correct individual, follow through on requests, and take care of the normal details of meeting dates and times. In emergencies, the secretary must contact a pastor to cover the congregation on a contingency basis.

None of these duties is spelled out in a job description. Yet, they are assumed by the congregation. If something happens to the pastor, lay people are assigned to answer the administrative questions, but the details are given to the secretary by default.

If for no other reason than to protect both the congregation and the secretary in situations when there is no pastor, it is necessary to have written policies and procedures. These must be standardized because several people might be filling the position of secretary when there is no pastor. Also, standardized procedures allow church leaders, including pastors, to maintain a normal operation when the secretary is gone.

CHAPTER 3

FUNCTIONS, FILING, AND FINDING

A significant difference between church and business offices is the kind of product behind the office. The church has nothing to sell; it is committed to a specific message and a way of life. The church is in the people business. As one of the most visible employees of the church, the secretary is a personification of the message and way of life the church hopes to express. Thus, a church secretary can hinder or help a congregation's outreach just by doing her or his job. This happens whether or not the secretary is a member of the congregation.

Being a church secretary is not a job for just anyone. It is a ministry. It is for this reason that a church secretary should not view the position merely as an occupation. One doesn't acquire the normal skills of a secretary in order to work for the church. Indeed, learning about and meeting its special demands are never completed. It is a profession into which one grows. To be effective a person must continually upgrade her or his skills, only a few of which are concerned with the use of office machines.

A church secretary's most important skills are people related. The church secretary who likes people and can discipline herself or himself to get tasks done on time and in excellent fashion is an asset to a congregation.

On a more personal note, it is important for church

secretaries to understand whom they work for. In many situations, accountability is directly to a pastor. In other congregations, a secretary may be hired by a pastor but be accountable to a committee of church members. No matter to whom they are accountable, church secretaries are open to criticism from every church member. The church secretary lives in a multi-faceted world of expectations and attitudes. Understanding the nature of this diversity is critical for a church secretary who intends to do a good job.

Functions

The church secretary performs several crucial functions. One of the most important is being a buffer between pastor and people. The secretary often needs to protect the pastor's time. This is especially important when the pastor regularly schedules time for study, worship preparation, and counseling. This function, when done with tact and firmness, can improve the quality of pastoral services.

Another church secretarial function is to help people gain access to the pastor. This requires a secretary to distinguish casual and nuisance calls from those which need a quick response. To perform this function well, a church secretary must be sensitive to the personal situations and needs of parishioners.

In addition to being a buffer and an interceder, the secretary functions as a guardian. The secretary, whether or not there is an official policy, decides who may use office machines and audiovisual equipment and have access to any of the files. A related task is to make certain that official congregational documents are kept in a safe place.

One of the more common duties of a secretary is being in charge of filing documents, minutes, and other records. A filing system is only as good as the ease of retrieval of materials from it. The retrieval system used must produce instant results no matter who is using it. This means the secretary must devise and maintain a foolproof filing and retrieval procedure.

A very important function is to handle a variety of people and their demands. The people with whom the secretary deals are a mixture of professionals, vendors, service people, sextons, visitors, and church members. The church secretary must be quite skilled in handling this variety of humans and their pressing demands. This means a church secretary is expected to be understanding and helpful while keeping to the normal tasks of the office.

This suggests that a church secretary should have better relational skills than the average secretary. If there is to be a trade-off between skill and relational qualifications, the emphasis must be on dealing with humans. Other skills can be improved. Liking to be with and work with people is a requirement for church secretaries.

Another important function is giving advice, usually to the pastor or volunteers. This may be preceded by doing research in order to be able to provide useful suggestions. In addition, a church secretary suggests the need for and may purchase equipment, supplies, and office materials.

The secretary, in some instances, will assist a committee or a pastor in selecting furniture for the office. In most places, a secretary must arrange an office to expedite work and make certain it and its machines are maintained. This chore is not glamorous but it is essential to the effectiveness of pastor, volunteers, and secretary.

Giving informal personal counsel to visitors and callers to the office is expected of most secretaries. A temptation in giving this advice is to go beyond the needs of the caller. Care must be taken in listening to the request and the background of the need. Then, counsel must be carefully given but should not assume more information than was given by the caller or visitor.

These are not the total functions of a church secretary but are very important ones. When being a secretary is considered a part of one's personal ministry, this position must be viewed as a caring and supportive activity. Being an evangelist and a disciplinarian must be reserved for other times.

Files and Filing

One of the most important and least rewarding secretarial tasks is keeping files. As suggested earlier, a church filing procedure has to be simple and self-evident because others may need to try to find something when the secretary isn't available.

Most people think of a filing system as being in file cabinets. This is generally the case, but church files may be in books, on computer tapes or disks, or, in the case of audiovisual resources, in special cabinets. While most files are in the church office, some documents may be in the custody of a bank or a lawyer and others may be in a bank vault or safety deposit box.

With regard to filing cabinets, some congregations use a single cabinet for storing current files regardless of type. This may necessitate the use of several drawers. The secretary would treat this cabinet as though it were several cabinets. This is done by using prominent dividers between each kind of file and clearly labeling both the drawers and the files.

A brief description outlining the manner of filing should be attached to the outside of each file cabinet. This ensures relatively easy access to the cabinet's contents. As a substitute for this method or to improve on it, an insert sheet in the front of each file drawer could tell what's in it. Both methods require a backup of the information. The backup, a file folder or a single page encased in a plastic protector, should be clearly marked and easily accessible to anyone who may need the information quickly. Usually the backup is kept on the secretary's desk top.

Church leaders need to use several types of files regularly. Therefore, the filing system must be built to accommodate their use rather than for other purposes. If this results in locating several file cabinets along a wall rather than having a nice table with magazines in that space, the files take precedence. Aesthetics are important but, in the church, functionality is more important.

Some files may be in books. These are easy to add to a system. They can be labeled, numbered, and shelved in a convenient location. Although the labels should be self-explanatory, an interpretative or master list which explains this part of the filing system should be kept.

Book files are widely used in churches for financial records and official minutes of congregational meetings. Because of their compactness and form they are easy to store in a locked room or closet. The key to the room or closet is handled by the secretary who gives it only to properly elected individuals of the congregation.

A few church files may be important enough to be kept in a protected place such as in a bank vault or by a lawyer. Usually these are legal and financial documents such as deeds, stocks, bonding papers, and the like. A record of what is in the vault or in the hands of a lawyer, who in the congregation can get access to the records, and when the items were placed there is a joint responsiblity of the trustees and the secretary. While the secretary doesn't make decisions about what should be put into the vault or who has access to those items, the secretary, to maintain a functional filing system for the church, must know where all the records are kept.

In some churches, financial and giving records may be on computer tapes at the bank. The secretary should know the proper contact for having bank records released and the individuals in the church who have responsibility for reading those records.

When the church has a computer the secretary should be the computer operator. This means the computer should be located in the church office so that the secretary controls computer use as well as access by others to records that might contain confidential information.

With the increasing numbers of churches that have personal computers in their offices, more and more records will be stored on disks. It is the secretary's responsibility to keep these in a safe place, to have backup copies available, and to have them properly and clearly labeled. Even though disks are small and contain much information, they are easy to copy, to destroy, and to take. Since church records are not for public consumption, the secretary must devise a method for ensuring that only those who are authorized have access to the computer and computer files.

In addition to regular files are resource files. These include copies of church school materials, book catalogs, and audiovisual samples. The secretary in a large congregation may not be responsible for such files, but in many congregations the secretary must take care of them. These should be separate from other files because they will be used by several people. For example, church school curriculum resources must be available to church school teachers and leaders. When these are kept in a separate file, the teachers do not have to bother the secretary unless they need to place an order.

Filing is not as easy as many people think. However, it can be made relatively simple by separating files into distinct groups. A description of these various kinds of files can help a secretary be more organized when handling this essential office procedure.

Types of Files

A church, no matter what its size, has several kinds of documents that must be saved and filed. While the number of the documents vary, the types are similar. These include: (1) legal documents; (2) membership, baptism, death, and marriage records; (3) financial records and, in many churches, individual giving records; (4) historical documents; (5) current program information; and (6) general files including correspondence, lists of vendors, calendars of meetings, officers, and the like. Each type of file is part of an interlocking system of records essential to the life and well-being of a congregation. While the contents of each file are distinctive, the files refer to one another and often are used in conjunction.

For instance, a proposed action of the trustees may involve checking in the legal file, searching through historical documents, and perusing materials in the general file before the action can be finalized. Cross-checking of a similar nature may be needed to verify a baptism, for example, that occurred some years ago. This means some method for correlating the files must be part of the total system. Usually this consists of a record of what is kept where in the files.

1. Legal Documents

Deeds, contracts, mortgages, and wills that name the church as beneficiary are among the legal documents a church collects over time. Some of these may be kept by the church's lawyer. Even so, the church should retain a duplicate copy in a legal file. This makes it possible to refer to the documents when necessary. Legal documents are needed, for instance, if a building program is being contemplated.

As a precaution, all church legal documents should be duplicated. The original may be put in a bank safety deposit box, and the duplicate can be retained in the church's office file. A record of all legal documents, originals and duplicates, should be kept by the secretary. This record can be made available to authorized persons in the congregation when requested or needed.

2. Membership, Baptism, Marriage, Death Records

The church is a people-centered institution; therefore, its records deal with events in people's lives. From the perspective of the church the most important of these is the membership record, i.e., who belongs and when they joined.

Maintaining up-to-date membership files is usually a task shared by the church secretary and the pastor. The secretary's part of the job is to make certain an accurate, current, and complete membership file is available at all times. Such a file is critical to the life and outreach of a congregation.

The most useful membership file tells at a glance which persons are immediate members of a family, which persons live close by, which are away from home temporarily (in school, in service, or on company assignment), the approximate age of each family member, and the date and manner by which they joined this chuch.

A separate file is kept for baptisms, another for marriages, and another for deaths, although this information is noted beside the appropriate members in the membership file. One reason for keeping a complete record of each of these types of events is that the church ministers to those who are not members. Parents may ask a pastor to baptize their child even though the parents are not members of the church. Since the baptism occurs in the church, the record is kept there.

Some pastors keep personal records of individuals they have baptized, those for whom they conduct marriages, and those for whom they perform funerals. This does not relieve the church of its responsibility for maintaining its own records of such events even when the people are not members. The services are performed by the pastor, who is an employee of the congregation. Eventually the pastor will leave. Over the long term, it is the church's institutional records to which people will refer.

Church secretaries should not hesitate to enter the names of persons involved in such services. The date and place of each event and those involved should be part of the record. Ages are appropriate as well. These files are as important as legal documents and can be used as such in some instances. Duplicates of these files are appropriate. Also, keeping the records in a safe place is essential.

3. *Financial and Individual Giving Files*

The treasurer's and auditor's records are usually kept by the treasurer with a copy in the church office. In addition to those of the church's general treasurer there may be financial records of the church school, the trustees, the youth, the choir, the women's groups, and the men's clubs. At least annual reports from each group having financial dealings in the name of the church should be part of the financial files.

Individual giving records are kept by a financial secretary in most congregations. These records are updated whenever an individual contributes to the church or one of its programs. Such records are confidential in most churches and are kept separate from other current church files. The church secretary's responsibility toward these files is to know who is in charge of them and who is authorized to examine them. In some churches, the files are kept under lock in the office with the secretary in charge of the key.

Financial and giving records can be classified as legal documents for some purposes. This is especially true when individuals need proof of their gifts to the church. Although the church secretary is not privy to information about any specific individual, it is the secretary's responsibility to make certain the files are kept in a safe and secure place.

4. *Historical Records*

Documents from the financial, current program, and general files can be classified as historical after two years. When a file is transferred to the historical file, two copies of most items are sufficient as records. These may be separated into duplicate files as a safeguard, but this may be too time consuming for most secretaries.

Copies of bulletins, newsletters, and program announcements need to be accessible since they can be used in current program planning. They may have historical value but are useful for some current needs. On the other hand, minutes of official congregational actions, including trustee and finance records, are important historically but tend not to be examined often. They need to be clearly labeled and stored in an accessible, but relatively fireproof place.

5. Current Program

These files will probably duplicate those maintained by the chairpersons of the various committees of the congregation. Included will be files on evangelism, education, missions, worship, choirs, outreach, pastoral relations, and other committees or groups authorized by and working on behalf of the congregation. Some of the information may be confidential and will be separated from the other file contents.

These files will be kept in the office with minimal supervision by the secretary. Each committee's secretary will be responsible for updating that committee's file. This does not relieve the church secretary from reminding those secretaries to regularly update their files.

Current program files are very important. The pastor and church leaders will need to use them regularly for planning and reference purposes. They will be referred to for annual reports and congregational meetings. Even though the church secretary is not responsible for maintaining the files, it is this person's duty to keep reminding the appropriate people to keep them up to date.

6. General Files

The general files of a congregation should tell an individual what is happening in the church. Included will be a list of church officers, committee personnel, a calendar of events, a list of current members by name and address, correspondence, and similar materials. Those items necessary to keep the church going are in this file.

The church secretary is the keeper of the general file. Decisions about where the material is to be put are made by the secretary. The file may take several forms, although the basic material is kept together. For example, a vendor list might be in a file folder as well as in a special telephone directory. A calendar of events may be in a list in a file folder as well as on a wall calendar displayed in the office. No matter how many places pieces of the file are found, the secretary is in charge of its accuracy.

7. *Pastor's Personal File*

This is not identified as one of the types of files of a congregation because it isn't a church file. It is a distinctly personal file relating to and maintained by a pastor. Even though a pastor may want to intermingle personal and church matters, the church secretary can insist on their separation. From the standpoint of a church, the pastor's personal file is a temporary record only for the benefit of the pastor.

The pastor's file will include personal correspondence, confidential items such as notes for counseling sessions, visitation records and notes, sermon ideas and illustrations, and personal calendars. Some of the material, such as the pastor's calendar, will be duplicated for the church secretary when it involves the pastor's work time. However, most of the pastor's file is of a personal nature.

A church secretary is hired to handle church matters and is not responsible for doing personal filing or personal errands for the pastor. A session to discuss this distinction should be a priority during the initial meeting between the church secretary and a pastor.

Finding

Creating and maintaining a rational filing process is the beginning of a file system. Equally important is building a retrieval procedure that finds information quickly. Without a good retrieval process, a filing system is useless.

Humans forget things quickly and can't remember when they need to the most. Therefore, a church secretary, as keeper of the files, must conceive of a plan to make remembering easy and finding things a simple task. This begins with organizing the system so that what goes into any file is listed on a master form located on a desk and available to those needing to use file materials.

1. A Master List

The master list will have the six headings for types of files that were just discussed. Under each heading, the documents in the file will be listed. For instance, under "Current Program," one of the items may be "Evangelism—Minutes." Beside this will be an entry telling what items are in that file. This might be a date such as "Jan. 1983–current," or it might be a special item identifying a specific event or emphasis such as "Lay Witness Retreat 10/22/84." The idea behind the master list is to enable the user to find a specific item quickly on demand.

Of course, a master list may be as elaborate as one desires. In some congregations, each type of file may have a summary list on a single page with references to additional pages which contain the details of what is found in each file folder or book. Such a list is very important for computer disks, which may contain several types of files on each disk.

A church secretary, in constructing the master list, will need to balance detail against quick access. There is a point at which detail confuses more than it helps. Note also that the list, including details, has to be updated whenever anything is added to the files. Consider this when thinking about adding complexity to a master list.

The master list is to be used for convenience and rapid retrieval. Since this is its purpose, a church secretary must tailor the list to meet these needs.

The master list must identify the place where a person can find the file cabinet, shelf, or office in which a particular item is stored. Sometimes a color code is used, but this is effective only when it is explained or self-evident. In creating a list, a secretary should never assume anything about someone else's memory, intelligence, or agility.

The master list should clearly show files that require special permission for access. These would include counseling appointments, visitation records, giving information, and other such items. In addition to noting the fact that they are confidential or limited, the list should, by symbol or office, show the person or persons who are authorized to have access, or who can authorize access, to each file. Having the names of these individuals along with their telephone numbers can save valuable time during emergency situations.

2. *Labeling*

Every file folder, book, or other container of material should clearly state what it contains. This should include, where appropriate, dates, events, and type of item. For instance, the correspondence files, since there may be several, may be "General, Jan.–June, 1983" or perhaps

"Vendors, Office Machines, Jan.–Dec., 1983" or "Trustees, Building Program, Jan.–Dec., 1983."

These illustrations show how labeling can result in quick and usable separation of correspondence related to program or other items by year and subject matter. Of course, these examples must be adjusted according to the needs of specific churches. In many congregations years may be combined or there may be multiple subjects in a single file. The degree of detail generally is determined by the size of the congregation.

Office-supply businesses offer several types of color-coded labels for files and for computer disks. It is possible to have the same color and type of label for folders and disks when the subject matter is complementary or when the material in the folder is a backup of a computer disk. In most instances color coding is quite effective. Similar files are quickly identifiable, and more specific identification then becomes a matter of reading the labels.

Books and cabinets should be labeled with the same sort of detail as file folders and computer disks. It is possible to add such things as page or shelf numbers to labels of books and cabinets.

Labeling of file cabinets is done in two places. The first is in the space allotted on the front of the drawer. This label tells the general content of the file. A second, more detailed label may be inside the drawer at the front. This tells specifically what is in the drawer. Instead of placing this as an insert in the drawer, some secretaries prefer using a self-adhesive label on the outside. In either case, the secretary must keep the label up to date in order for it to be useful.

3. *Most-Used Items*

One portion of a file system might be devoted to items that are used often by a variety of people—for example, lists of officers or lists of members. The intent is to have at one's fingertips those names, actions, or telephone numbers most often requested.

Deciding what goes into this part of the file is difficult. A person's tendency is to make it too large. At most, it should be no more than half a dozen folders in the front part of a cabinet or in a desk drawer. The secretary is in charge of it and decides what goes in it. The materials are duplicates of items found in other parts of the filing system. No originals should be in this file.

Each item in this part of the file should note where similar or backup information may be found. Thus, if a pastor uses the file when the secretary isn't in, the pastor can easily find additional reference materials.

Summary

The functions of a secretary range from keeping the office functioning to advising pastors, committees, and individuals on matters related to the church and its programs. These duties demand an individual who is willing to keep on learning, who likes people, and who can tolerate stress.

Churches have multiple types of files, each of which should be distinctive but interrelated to the others. Knowing what these types are and where they are located is a major responsibility of the secretary.

A filing system is no better than its means for retrieval. The use of color codes, labeling, and a "most-used" section in the filing of materials makes retrieval easy and rapid. Decisions about both filing and retrieval can be made by the secretary, but a guide for use of the system must be available, easy to understand, and up to date.

CHAPTER 4

TELEPHONE

The telephone has revolutionized the work of the church. It has become the vital link between members and clergy, leaders and the church office, and people needing information or help. It is used to enlist volunteers, to keep track of the sick and invalids, to be in touch with people who need to be aware of administrative details of the church, and to promote programs.

The importance and versatility of the telephone are sometimes overlooked by secretaries. It is viewed by them as a necessary evil when it interrupts their work. At other times it is a tyrant because it seems to be tied up at the times when they desperately need it to get something done. However, secretaries are aware of its benefits. They are the first to reach for it when a problem arises. It is their connection to service people and to those in authority who can find money for urgent repairs or replacements of machines and supplies.

Church people, secretaries included, because they use the telephone so much in their family and business, don't think about using it carefully. People forget that a church telephone can be an image builder or an image destroyer. It can be a link or an obstruction between the church and people. Which of these it becomes depends on the way the telephone is used. Good manners, warmth, and careful listening convey one type of church, while poor manners and nonchalance tell the caller negative things about a church.

The way a telephone is used, the tone of voice, the kind of replies a caller receives, the manner in which information is given or received, and the promptness of returning calls, give people, members and outsiders, clues as to the nature of the office and the church. "Having a bad day" is not an acceptable excuse for poor telephone techniques. A caller who is greeted on an early morning by a surly tone may be an individual who needs help. The tone of the reply will tell the person not to expect help from that church. This perception is picked up from the attitude of the church person answering the telephone.

Who uses the telephone is another issue in most congregations. Not only is it available to secretaries, it must be used by volunteers, leaders, pastors, and others for a variety of things. Who pays for these calls? Who keeps the records? These and other issues regarding telephone use can cause unnecessary conflicts.

Just as important as the manner of use of the telephone is its location. If the telephone is shared by the pastor's family and the church office, special agreements about its use need to be fashioned.

These items are raised in the following discussion. While not every issue related to telephone use in a specific congregation may be dealt with, the method for handling various issues will be clear.

Answering the Telephone

Answering the telephone begins with greetings and ends with good-byes, but, for the church, telephone use includes making records of calls and taking messages. A pleasant tone of voice, stable temperament, and the ability to function when someone is angry, abusive, or experiencing a crisis are important characteristics for someone constantly answering the telephone. It makes no difference who initiates the call or why, these elements must be considered.

1. Greetings

Every secretary learns quickly to read the attitude of the boss by the tone of her or his voice at the beginning of the day. This mood may be revealed by the way he or she says "hello" or by the fact that instead of words the boss grunts a welcome. If the secretary can read the boss's feelings that quickly, then obviously it is just as easy for a caller to read the secretary's attitude by a greeting on the telephone. People can't see smiles on faces, but they can hear when smiles or grunts appear. The way people are greeted will affect the outcome of the conversation.

The greeting of a telephone caller is more than a pleasant "hello" to an effective secretary. It conveys a tone about the church, it screens the caller, it gives information, and it gives the secretary an opportunity to reschedule a call at a time when the caller's request can be handled more readily. A church secretary should not confuse the answering of the church telephone with the more informal greetings used on a home phone to talk with family or relatives.

The astute secretary understands the importance of the greeting not only as the beginning but as the shaper of conversations. For instance, greetings can be used to screen callers. A courteous, businesslike approach can discourage the nuisance caller, the random-call sales pitch, and the time wasters. The success of each of these types of calls depends on the telephone answerer's willingness to spend time on nonessentials. A businesslike approach which includes the ability to say "no" or "not interested" or "I'm too busy now" can effectively relieve a secretary and a pastor from calls that might be interesting but not useful.

Greetings may be combined with specific requests such as "How may I help you?" While the phrase used may vary from church to church, the message is the same. The secretary is telling the caller that he or she is ready to try to satisfy a request. This may startle the caller, but it makes conversation easier than a mere "hello."

Greetings should include some information so the caller knows he or she has reached the correct number. The name of the church and the name of the secretary ought to be given as part of the greeting. These bits of information are processed by the caller, and a conversation may be terminated by "Sorry, wrong number." If the number is correct, the caller knows who is answering the telephone and can move from that point to her or his need.

Occasionally, the caller is hostile and angry about something the pastor or a church leader has said or done. The secretary's greeting, pleasant though it may be, can be overwhelmed by the caller's anger. The secretary must maintain her or his calm by remembering that anger is not dealt with effectively by answering anger. Hostility is not an option for a church secretary.

It is appropriate for a church secretary to ask the individual to call back when he or she has had an opportunity to cool down. Another version of this tactic may be a suggestion by the secretary that the person call back in a few minutes in order for the secretary to be better prepared to handle the complaint. During the interval, the secretary will need to look up data about the complaint and decide on several alternative actions. Buying time, which is what the secretary is doing, gives the caller a chance to become more rational and allows the secretary to prepare emotionally and factually for an obvious encounter.

An evaluation for a secretary might include random recordings of her or his telephone greetings. People slip into habits. Randomly recording greetings can highlight unconscious mannerisms on the telephone which may be telling callers that the office isn't interested in talking to them, that the secretary is too busy to be bothered, that messages won't be relayed, or that this is an alive and dynamic place.

2. *Good-bye*

The way in which a conversation is ended is probably more important than its beginning. A poor beginning may be offset by a good conversation, but a dismal ending cannot be repaired. The final impression a caller has is left by the last comments or good-byes of the secretary.

The good-bye needs to combine a personal and a business ending. For instance, "I'll give this message to Pastor Will as soon as she comes in. Meanwhile, have a good day," is one way to conclude a routine conversation. It tells the caller that the secretary will do what has been requested, and it expresses a good feeling.

An ending to a hostile call needs to be more businesslike. It may include a personal wish so long as it is uplifting. For instance, such a call might be ended by, "I'll bring this matter to the attention of Mr. Johns of the Trustees by telephone later today. I will request him to be in touch with you. In addition, I will send you a note confirming these agreements. Thank you for bringing this to our attention." Something like this is strictly business, although the last phrase is equivalent to a personal ending.

A wrong number can be irritating and time consuming. For example, a church's number was one digit different from that of a glass company. The secretary got at least one call each week from someone needing replacement panes for windows or doors. Her inclination was to let her irritation show, but she decided accidents, such as reading or dialing the wrong digit, happen to everyone. She accepted the wrong numbers as part of a normal day at the office. Her greetings took care of most of them, and a few questions from the caller when she answered gracefully handled the remainder.

Once in a while a conversation degenerates in spite of everything a secretary can do. When this happens the caller may slam the telephone down in anger or disgust. The end to the call is so abrupt the secretary has not been able to terminate it in a normal fashion. The best thing to do in such instances is to try to forget about it.

In some cases, a follow-up call on another day to ask about requests or to answer a criticism may be appropriate. Such follow-ups ought not to be attempted when the content of the first call was emotional and without a factual base. There is no good response to a wholly emotional tirade about a church or a church leader.

3. *Records*

It's a nuisance to keep records. Yet, most people who talk on the telephone are scribbling notes as they talk. Translating this tendency into a system to record telephone calls can do the secretary and the pastor much good. A secretary, to convert scribbles into usable records, needs only to jot down the name and general content of a conversation to have a record. When this is done regularly, the church office can detect patterns, including types of calls and frequency of calls from specific persons.

Frequent requests of a particular nature may signal a need for new types of brochures or printed information. For instance, a church secretary notices at the end of two months that several visitors to the community have called to ask about the time of Sunday services. The outside bulletin board is evidently not reaching these people. It isn't enough advertising. The secretary alerts the pastor and administrative committee of an apparent need and suggests a weekly ad in the newspaper and a listing of worship times in the telephone book. Without an accurate record of telephone calls, the church might never have become aware of this need or been able to do anything about it.

Keeping records of telephone calls can alert a pastor to a personal or family need within the parish. In one parish the secretary noticed that a young mother was calling the office about every other day with some request. The secretary alerted the pastor to these calls after two weeks and suggested that the woman might need a visit. Although this family was not on the "to be visited" list for another month, the pastor called on the woman within the week. She was an emotional wreck because her sister had been diagnosed as having a very serious disease. The pastor was able to assist her because of the secretary's record keeping.

Not every secretary's record of telephone calls will have such dramatic results. On the other hand, neither of these secretaries felt their keeping records of telephone calls was anything more than pure drudgery. Only after being able to see results did they understand the importance of recording telephone calls.

A telephone call record is very simple to keep. It can be a page for each day, week, or month. Forms may be constructed by the secretary which contain the date, time, person's name, and call content. Such a form might look like this:

Telephone Record: Week of____________________

Date	Time	Name	Content
_____	_______	_______________	__________________

The exact size of the paper and the amount of space for each item will depend on the secretary. There should be enough margin on the left so that the sheets may be punched and put into a binder for safekeeping. Confidential notes and messages related to specific calls will be filed elsewhere. This is strictly a record of telephone calls. However, the call record should not be open to general inspection. It is a tool that can be useful for the pastor and the secretary.

4. *Messages*

Taking messages is an art that necessitates good handwriting and accuracy. A message also demands careful listening. Finally, a message is not worth anything until it is delivered and acted upon.

Every telephone should have beside it a blank piece of paper (a pad of paper is appropriate in most offices) and a pencil or pen that writes. Where there is no secretary a sign next to the telephone can instruct whoever answers the telephone to get the name, telephone number, and message of the caller so a return call might be made. It would help to include the date and time of the call, so the pastor or other person who must return the call will know when it was received.

Because the caller will speak more rapidly than the message taker can write down what is said, it is important to read back information that is to be included in a message. Repeating the telephone number (numbers are hard to catch the first time through) and the message can clarify the intent of the person leaving the data.

Sometimes callers do not want to leave their names and telephone numbers. The fact that they called should be noted on the message pad along with information that they will call back or that the item isn't important enough to leave a message. This notation will indicate to the individual to whom it is directed that someone called and may be calling back later.

A very frustrating experience occurs when one leaves a message and receives no return call. Many business people expect no follow-up, so they are in a habit of calling again if they haven't received a response within a few hours' time. This is a bother to the business people as well as to the secretary, who may or may not be at fault.

The obligation of a secretary taking a message is to get that information to the proper person in as short a time as possible. Merely placing a message on the pastor's desk is not enough. Talking to the pastor about the message and handing it to her or him is a much better procedure. That way the urgency of a call can be transmitted as well as more information than is included in the note.

A secretary who takes a message just before leaving for the day thinks it is enough to put it in the pastor's office or on the desk. It is appropriate to do those things and, in addition, to make a note to herself or himself to check with the pastor the next morning about what action has been taken on the message. A message is not really dealt with until it has resulted in some action.

Occasionally, a message is left for the secretary. It makes sense to call the individual who left the message to clarify what is needed and then to fill the request. There is nothing wrong with verifying messages. Indeed, such follow-ups can save a great deal of time and energy.

Use of the Church Telephone

Churches need a policy or general office practice to define who may use the telephone and under what circumstances. Usually, offices do not allow secretaries or employees to utilize the telephone for personal calls or business. Neither do offices let nonemployees use the telephone unless it is an emergency or is a credit-card call. These procedures can be followed most of the time in business offices, but the church is different.

Church offices are there to serve people, especially members. While a church may have a policy or general practice, it is unlikely the secretary will be able to rigidly enforce the policy or practice. Certain leaders and individuals are exceptions to every rule, especially in the church. Who these are will be known to a secretary and, if not, to the pastor, who will inform the secretary.

Use of the church telephone should be limited to business essential to the church. There are occasions, however, when personal calls are necessary and individuals in the church need to use the telephone for a specific reason. Church secretaries must be flexible enough to allow limited use for personal needs while maintaining enough control to deny use to people who will unnecessarily tie up the telephone.

If the church office force is volunteer, a strict accounting of telephone use will curtail much of the unnecessary calling. In such offices an individual could be assigned to monitor telephone use. However, a monitor who is self-appointed will create more problems than he or she can solve.

When a church telephone is to be used regularly in a program, such as daily checking of elderly persons, another line with an extension telephone should be installed. A program telephone has a different function from a regular office phone. Program calling is done by volunteers or a particular staff member. Having this line attached to the secretary's telephone may be useful, although answering it could become a problem. An alternative is to attach the program telephone to an answering machine when no one related to the program is available.

A church office with a part-time secretary (volunteer or paid) may want to invest in an answering machine. Some people don't like to talk to a machine, but it is better than losing calls. The message is as clear as the caller makes it, and, if the machine is checked each evening, messages will get to the designated individual within a few hours. Most people prefer this alternative to not getting through at all.

Instructions about recording calls and taking messages should be given to each person who works in the office, volunteer or employee. These instructions should be put by each telephone in the church. Next to these instructions should be an information sheet that details expected telephone use for that congregation. Such a sheet would identify the kinds of calls that may be made, payment for those calls, and authorization procedures for making calls other than those listed.

A church with multiple telephone lines needs to decide which are direct to offices and which should be connected through a secretary. Part of this consideration will be who pays for the program or staff member with direct lines. For instance, some churches house community groups that have a part-time or volunteer director. These groups generally have their own telephone and are responsible for managing it without the assistance of the church secretary.

It is reasonable to expect a church secretary to be in charge of most of the calls coming into the church. This doesn't mean the secretary will have to monitor all the calls out of the church. Her or his responsibility for the telephone, unless a specific decision has been made to change the duties of the secretary, is to record incoming calls and to make those calls necessary for fulfilling her or his duties.

Church and Parsonage Phone Arrangements

Small-membership congregations often have a telephone in the church with an extension to the parsonage (or vice versa), or they have a telephone in the parsonage without a phone in the church building. Either of these arrangements puts people who call in direct contact with the pastor. Without such an arrangement people often can't get in touch with the pastor because he or she is not at the church much of the time.

But the main problem with having the telephone in the parsonage is that anyone who is in the church building can't use it without bothering the family. Worse yet, they may not be able to use it at all during an emergency, either because the family is out or the telephone is tied up by another caller. This leaves the alternative of finding another telephone, and this may be difficult or impossible.

Another problem with having the telephones only in the parsonage is that messages often aren't taken or given to the proper party. Young children may be left at home and may take telephone calls when parents are gone, with the result that important messages can be waylaid or mislaid, with the result that nothing happens. That's OK for many kinds of messages, but it could be tragic for another type.

It is very important, therefore, for volunteers or the administrative committee of the congregation to instruct parsonage families in proper telephone procedures. It may seem out of place for church people to be teaching a pastor and her or his family how to use a telephone, but it is proper and essential. The church functions because of lay persons, and they need to be able to work through the pastor. That work often is conducted by telephone; at the very least, appointments to do the work are made by telephone. If the pastor's family doesn't know how to use the telephone, take messages, keep records, and pass messages to the correct people, the church is hurt more than the pastor.

Churches that share a telephone with the pastor need to have guidelines for answering it. For example, a church secretary may be in the church two mornings a week. During those times, she or he should be responsible for handling calls, taking messages, and passing those messages to the right person. During the remainder of the week, the pastor, a member of the pastor's family, or an answering machine will be taking the calls.

Sharing a telephone between the church and the parsonage can create unnecessary tensions. The pastor's private life can be greatly disrupted by a church telephone. This disruption may be caused by a large number of calls from parishoners, or it may be a result of the pastor using the telephone for personal business. In order to avoid tensions, a congregation and a pastor need to develop guidelines by which both can live with regard to telephone use.

In most settings, it would be worth the money to have separate telephones for the church and for the parsonage or pastor. It is difficult enough to work with a telephone in the church without adding the troubles created by party lines (which is the same as sharing a telephone between church and pastor).

The responsibility for recommending separate telephones and drawing up guidelines for use in shared situations rests with an administrative committee of the church. This committee will need information about telephone use in the church. These data can be supplied by volunteers, a secretary, or persons caring for the secretarial roles in a church. The data would come from a record of telephone calls.

It would be inaccurate to suggest that a church will decide to give up an arrangement it has lived with for several years without careful consideration of hard data. These data can come only from records kept by people acting as secretaries.

The telephone is such an important part of church life that it needs much attention. Creating a little manual about how to answer it, use it, and share it should be a priority of administrative committees in all sizes of churches. It is an important tool and, when used constructively, can enhance the ministry of a church. Secretaries need to assist congregations in understanding its importance and proper use.

CHAPTER 5

EQUIPMENT

Office equipment includes typewriters, duplicating machines, dictating machines, recording equipment, overhead or other types of projectors, computers, printers, and calculators. This list is not exhaustive, but it provides a framework for the following discussion. Equipment, in the sense in which it is used here, refers to machines rather than file cabinets or storage cabinets and bookcases.

Poor or inoperable equipment makes an efficient and effective office an impossibility. Good equipment that is inadequately maintained causes frustration and conflict among those who must use it. People who work in an office but who don't know how to operate its equipment will ignore the machines and resort to their own devices to get work done. While it is important to have office equipment in churches, those machines must be well maintained and used properly. Otherwise, the machines become artifacts rather than tools.

Good equipment, by itself, can't make an office run efficiently. It must be taken care of, and supplies for it must be kept on hand. Otherwise, secretaries can be blamed for not having adequate supplies for the equipment, for poor oversight when equipment doesn't work, or for not giving proper training if volunteers or other office workers can't get equipment to operate properly. There are times when blame for lack of supplies and equipment maintenance is correctly placed on a secretary. However, in many situations the secretary should not be faulted. In these cases, the difficulties can be traced to the church's not providing enough money to see that supplies, maintenance, and training are taken care of.

Churches, if they want secretaries to function to their capabilities, must provide adequate budgets for equipment maintenance and supplies. Not only that, churches must insist that secretaries be trained to use office machines properly. Churches should require every secretary, paid and volunteer, to be trained to use each piece of equipment in the office.

Training is something to be provided by the church office; it cannot be expected that the secretary will come equipped with an operating knowledge of office machines. That's the reason churches should insist that any new person in the office be taught how to run all the office machines. Responsibility for enforcing this requirement rests with the church's administrative committee. When this group does its job well, secretaries learn to operate and maintain the equipment in the office.

Administrative committees realize quickly that money can't buy a secretary's willingness to learn new techniques. For instance, purchasing a dictating system will not mean that a secretary will use it. Neither does having money in the budget stimulate a secretary to buy equipment that could save time and effort. For example, having enough money to buy a computer, which could do many tasks more quickly than they are done otherwise, does not guarantee that one will be purchased or used.

Before they will use office equipment, secretaries have to be able to change their habits. They must be encouraged to learn how to utilize equipment that will relieve them of routine, time-consuming jobs. For example, a folding machine takes getting used to, but its output is fast and efficient.

Secretaries must be sent to training sessions to learn how to operate equipment. Most dealers offer training or orientation sessions for purchasers of machines. Many times these sessions are free. Learning to use a machine is an important first step in efficiency.

Secretaries need to be encouraged to research ways to improve office procedures and to suggest the purchase of equipment that will enable the church office to do its various jobs better. This doesn't mean a secretary must have unlimited funds. However, when an individual is encouraged to learn, the possibility of innovation and experimentation is greatly enhanced.

A secretary's attitude toward machines in the office is more important than the number and types of equipment. No machine will be useful or productive until the secretary decides it is something he or she can use to be effective and more productive. The efficient use of any piece of office equipment is dependent upon the attitude of the secretary. Often, it is the secretary's attitude which influences how well office equipment is maintained, the adequacy of office supplies, and the kinds of machines available in the office.

Warranties, Maintenance, and Repairs

Warranties are provided by equipment manufacturers. The warranty usually extends from three to twelve months from the date of purchase. Often, the warranty is good even if the machine has been purchased used. The warranty extends for the period specified in the original purchase document.

However, churches purchasing used machines should ask whether or not warranties are transferable or assumable.

Office equipment dealers generally offer maintenance contracts for what they sell. These contracts normally are for one year and are renewable. Since service contracts are optional, a secretary must ask for them. However, it is wise not to have a contract for a machine that is rarely used. The decision to get a contract should be based on use and past repair history for any given machine.

The procedure for securing a maintenance contract for a machine that was not purchased at a local supplier is to have the machine examined prior to issuing the contract. For example, a typewriter that is purchased used from a private party can be put under a maintenance contract after the dealer examines it and puts it in good working order. This preliminary work lets the dealer and the owner know the current condition of the equipment.

Finding a reliable repair or service company is a necessity. Equipment will need repairs. It is important to use a service company familiar with the particular kinds of equipment a church office has rather than calling a service person who has no particular specialty. Besides having experience and expertise in a particular line of equipment, a service company should offer a guarantee for its work; a normal guarantee is for three months.

If a piece of equipment is purchased through a mail-order house, a local or regional dealer who can service the equipment should be found. It is inconvenient, expensive, and time consuming to send equipment to a manufacturer's representative for repairs or service. It could be worth a few extra dollars at purchase time to buy a product with adequate local service facilities.

Proper equipment maintenance is the responsibility not of

a service company but of the secretary. This begins with the careful reading of owner manuals. They tell what the owner should do to keep the equipment in good working condition. None of these manuals should be thrown away as long as the equipment remains in the office or a store room of the church. A listing of the manuals and where they are kept should be made and filed in a readily accessible place.

Particularly important in maintenance is cleanliness. Regular cleaning of the equipment will save much grief. Dusting and vacuuming will keep dirt and paper particles from accumulating. Often these small pieces or scraps of paper get in the wrong places and jam machines. At least once a month, equipment should be cleaned thoroughly. The time spent will save frustration and lost time as well as repair costs.

Working Conditions

Offices in which machines are used need to be well decorated. This doesn't mean they should have lavish furnishings or the walls painted with decorator colors. Well decorated means that the walls are clean and painted (not papered) and the floor covering is in good condition. Worn carpets, unfinished floors, or rickety steps can cause serious injury to a secretary who is busy operating a machine. Disrepair, in addition to being dangerous, creates an attitude of not caring.

A church wishing to enhance office productivity will make certain the physical surroundings in which secretaries (paid or volunteer) work are clean, neat, and attractive. The willingness of an individual to use a machine is directly influenced by the attractiveness of the room in which the machine must be used. If the room is drab, below ground level, poorly lighted, and in need of renovation, people will not want to use the machine no matter how useful it is. People are attracted or repelled by the decor of a room. Therefore, when placing equipment in rooms or offices, a committee or the secretary should consider the psychological effect the room will have on the persons using the machine.

Adequate lighting and ventilation should be provided in rooms in which equipment is used. Accidents happen when people are made drowsy by chemicals or can't see well enough to safely operate machines. No matter which piece of office equipment is being used, the secretary should insist on good lighting and adequate ventilation. This latter may not be too important when using a calculator, but it is very important when using copying or duplicating machines. Good lighting and air circulation keep people alert. Being physically alert ensures better secretarial productivity.

Rooms where equipment is used should be kept clean. Paper, rags, or chemicals should not be allowed to accumulate. Not only are these potential hazards to an operator, they present a fire risk. As a precaution, fire extinguishers should be placed near duplicating equipment and other machines the operation of which or supplies for which could cause combustion.

In the case of computers and some duplicating machines, the office temperature has to be kept within a certain range. This will necessitate air conditioning and good air circulation. Most duplicating machines give off heat, and some means must be provided for keeping them at an operable temperature. Careful reading of the manuals can help ensure that adjustments are made to accommodate their needs. When church secretaries ignore the requirements of ventilation and temperature, machines don't function properly.

Basic Equipment

An office should not have more equipment than it needs to do its jobs well and on time. A church that grows from one hundred to five hundred members in three years doesn't need to outfit its office like a commercial firm. The church office doesn't have the same kinds of tasks to accomplish as a business. A church office's volume may increase because members are added but not by a great deal. The work of a church office is determined in large measure by the style of its ministry. Thus, the administrative committee should judge office equipment needs for its church by the work to be done, not by the size of its congregation.

A church office deals with people. This fact dictates the kind of equipment it should contain. The following types of equipment fill basic needs in church offices.

1. Typewriters

Typewriters may be manual, electric, or electronic. The price of a typewriter rather than its capabilities may determine which is purchased and used. However, churches with at least one secretary (paid or volunteer) should invest in a good electric typewriter. It is faster and more versatile than most manual typewriters.

Some churches have both an electric and a manual typewriter. The manual typewriter is used for a particular purpose, such as doing stencils for bulletins or as a backup for the electric machine. The electric typewriter is used for all typing other than stencils.

The electronic typewriter may be more appropriate for larger congregations. It has memory capacities and can be used to produce print-ready brochures, newsletters, and bulletins. However, its capabilities can be overshadowed by a computer or word processor attached to a letter quality printer. A computer and printer may be in the same price range as an electronic typewriter. Also, some computers may use electronic typewriters as printers.

No matter which kind or combination is chosen, there have to be enough typewriters to do office work efficiently. If an office has three secretaries, it will need at least two typewriters (one secretary may be engaged for bookkeeping, filing, and duplicating). Scheduling office hours on a staggered basis may be one solution to the problem of too few machines and not enough budget to purchase more. This can be done with volunteers or paid personnel. For example, typing work can be done in the evening or on Saturday by secretaries as well as on weekdays.

2. *Duplicating Machines*

Church offices need access to duplicating machines. They must have letters, bulletins, and notices copied and sent or distributed to members. The duplicating machines found most often in churches are mimeographs or copy machines, spirit-duplicating machines or small offset presses. The chances are that most congregations will have a mimeograph to handle their duplicating chores.

Some churches have a machine to make electronic stencils. This is viewed as a luxury item by most congregations, but it is very useful. With such a scanner a church office has more creative possibilities in designing duplicated materials than when regular stencils are used.

A few churches have replaced their mimeographs with copy machines. This alternative relieves secretaries of the mess of mimeograph ink and stencils. Duplicating is relatively simple when done by plain paper copiers. The quality of the copy varies with the type and condition of the machine. The initial investment in a copy machine may make this alternative attractive only to more affluent churches. The cost per page, however, can make copy machines a good buy.

The spirit duplicator has proved popular among churches. It uses an alcohol-based liquid to produce copies. It is simple to use and is good for up to 50 copies of an item. Some congregations use this type of duplicator exclusively because it is inexpensive and their needs are limited.

Duplicating machines may be used in combination. For example, a mimeograph might be used for bulletins, letters, or notices going to the entire congregation, while the spirit duplicator could be used for notices of meetings, a script for a children's play, or something with only a few copies.

3. *Telephone Equipment*

The type of telephone equipment needed is determined by the number of people who must use it. For example, if there is a full-time secretary and a full-time pastor, one phone line may be enough. When the number of people increase either in the office or on the staff, the number of telephone lines should increase. This often necessitates a more sophisticated central terminal which is located in the office. A telephone or communications company can assess needs and assist in selecting the appropriate service for a church.

4. *Dictating Machines*

Dictating equipment is an excellent substitute for hand-written notes and letters, which a secretary must transcribe and type. Dictating to a secretary using shorthand is a waste of person power. It ties up the secretary and the person doing the dictation at the same time. Usually much dictating time is given to thinking or to changing a letter or item. It makes much more sense to teach office people to use electronic dictating equipment than to spend time waiting for each other to write or to think. Using dictating equipment allows the secretary and the person doing the dictating to work on their own schedules.

A basic dictating system would be one machine with a microphone, an earphone, and a foot pedal. A more sophisticated system would include two units, one for dictating and one for transcribing. Either system is an improvement over shorthand dictation.

A dictating system can be useful in churches with part-time pastors. It can increase the productive power of a pastor who may leave tapes of instructions and work for a secretary (part or full time, paid or volunteer) to do on a daily or weekly basis. (A backup tape would provide copies of all instructions and work, although making a backup can be time consuming unless there is a tape duplicating machine handy.)

5. *Paper Handling Machines*

An electric stapler is a small machine but it is a time saver. The initial investment is slight when compared to the speed with which the time-consuming job of stapling is done. Of course, its purchase depends on the amount of paper work being processed by the office. In cases where volunteers are willing to give the time to office work, this tool lightens their load considerably.

Collators, either manual or electric, are essential in

churches where reports or minutes are more than a single page in length. The manual collator consists of a series of separators from which an individual selects one page at a time. Up to eighteen pages can be collated at once. A simple collating machine allows an operator to collect six pages at a time but does it faster than a manual collator. Sometimes a collator may be purchased for a copy machine. This allows a report or minutes to be copied and collated simultaneously.

A paper folder is an important labor saver for churches with several mailings per month. These machines can be used to fold bulletins as well. Usually this piece of equipment is well worth its cost in churches with a limited office corps and volunteers who do not like office work, as well as in offices with many mailings.

6. *Outside Jobber*

An alternative to purchasing any of these pieces of equipment is to have all or part of the office work done by outside jobbers. This might be a solution for small congregations that do not want to invest in equipment and/or who have no one interested in volunteering to do the work. There are low-cost printing/copying centers that offer to do typing, set-up of print and copy runs, and duplicating. These businesses cater to churches that do not want to invest in equipment, especially duplicating machines.

Even when a church decides to use outside jobbers to do much of its work, a secretary and a typewriter are essential. The secretary must type correspondence, file, and take care of the office. In addition, she or he has to set the material up, take it to the jobber, pick it up, and make certain it gets to the proper people. These are not the tasks a congregation pays a pastor to do. In such churches, a secretary must be willing to spend time with the jobber to ensure he or she understands what is being requested and in negotiating schedules and prices.

7. Scheduling, Placement, Insurance

No matter which pieces of equipment are purchased, the secretary is responsible for their use. This means, in some churches, scheduling machine use. When scheduling is necessary, priorities of use have to be established. For instance, materials for a meeting this week have higher priority than items announcing an event two months from now. Also, the weekly bulletin should have a specific duplication time.

Equipment needs to be placed in rooms where it can be used. Most equipment will not be in the main church office. Duplicating, folding, stapling, and cutting equipment should be in a room adjacent to the main office. This allows the secretary to monitor and schedule equipment use while working at a desk in the main office. Of course, dictating equipment will be close to the secretary. A dictating machine can be stored in a drawer in the desk or in a closed cabinet when not in use.

Office equipment should be kept in locked rooms. It is unpleasant to realize that people steal church items, but they do. Restrictions on moving or borrowing machines must be enforced. This is easier when they are kept in a locked room with a key in the care of a secretary.

As a matter of course, a church ought to carry insurance on all its office equipment. This insurance should be upgraded regularly to reflect the equipment in the office.

Number Machines

Every church office will have access to one or two calculators. The most common is an adding machine. Depending on its age, this machine may be partially manual with a small keyboard or it may be electronic with math functions built into it. In most cases, machines purchased within the past five years will have both printers and LED displays.

It isn't necessary to have number machines with several complicated mathematical functions or displays with more than eight digits. Purchasing calculators or adding machines with many other options increases the price but not the usefulness for the church. Churches deal with counting numbers and computing percentages. These common functions are found on most relatively inexpensive machines.

It is a good idea to buy calculators that are AC-powered. Hand-held and battery-powered calculators are nice for people who travel or who need to calculate figures on the spot. But most church secretaries can wait until they get to an electrical outlet to add costs, subtract items from an inventory, or calculate projected income and expenses.

Churches ought to have two different number machines. At least one should be a calculator, although both may be. When several people need to use a calculator on a regular basis a church should purchase more of them since they are inexpensive.

Computers

Churches that mail items regularly, keep records of income and expense, maintain membership lists, or use a pledge system should have a computer. A computer can be the most helpful piece of equipment used in church offices. It allows secretaries to do a lot of routine work easily and quickly. It computes and prepares financial reports in a fraction of the time normally given to typing them. It can print individualized letters and can produce address labels without having to enter the name or correction more than once.

On the other hand, computers take patience to learn how to use. A secretary must learn how to use the software (instructions for making the computer work properly) before any results of computer use will be evident. Learning how to use software takes time. Therefore, a church ought not to expect to get many results from a computer until the secretary has mastered some of its programs.

Programs most often used by congregations are those for keeping track of finances, recording pledges and sending pledge updates, keeping membership records, and using various word processing functions. (Word processing is writing, which includes correspondence.) Sophisticated data-base or financial spread-sheet programs are not needed generally, nor are they helpful. However, the church school may use Bible quizzes and simulation games designed for the computer.

Computer prices vary greatly. Therefore, it is wise to consult a book or two about what to look for when purchasing a computer before buying one. What is useful in a home setting is not always functional for a church. Neither is a computer designed for business the most appropriate kind for most churches. A congregation must determine what it is going to do now and in the future with a computer before it begins to get serious about a purchase.

Once a computer is purchased, serious attention must be

given to the kind of printer that will be used with it. The most appropriate kind of printer is a letter quality one. The difference in price between letter quality printers is due to their speed, i.e., the least expensive are the slowest. Speed is not essential since even the slowest of them is faster than a typist. In addition, because the material to be printed is stored in memory, the print-out is more accurate than copy prepared by most typists.

Many secretaries inaccurately assume that the computer is difficult to learn and will create many problems for them. Learning to use the computer will take time, but so did learning typing and shorthand. Everything related to machines takes time to understand. When a secretary begins to learn how to use a computer the church ought to allow three to five months for her or him to become comfortable with it.

A major problem with a computer is controlling its use. It should be placed in the secretary's control, although an additional computer may be in a pastor's office. (If there are two, they should be of the same kind so the software is compatible.) Strict control of who uses it for what is important.

Computers themselves will have few maintenance problems since there are no moving parts except the keyboard and switch. However, the monitor and disk drives are mechanical or easily breakable and must be carefully protected.

It is a good idea to purchase a cover for the machine. It is susceptible to dust and dirt. This is true of the printer as well. In addition, a printer is more easily tolerated in an office if it is enclosed with a sound-deadening cover.

Other Types of Equipment

A secretary may be caretaker and maintainer of audio-visual equipment. This may include video recorder, video camera, videotape, cassette recorders and tape, record players, slide projectors, and filmstrip projectors among other items. It may be up to the secretary to schedule the use of these things. Not often, however, would the secretary use them in her or his work.

If a secretary becomes custodian of audiovisual equipment, a careful inventory of existing items should be made. Then a form ought to be created which will itemize additional acquisitions. The secretary should then put an agreement into writing, stating that matters of depreciation, insurance, and replacement of these items are the responsibilities of the trustees or finance committee. In this way a secretary separates custodial equipment from those machines used regularly in the church office in fulfilling secretarial duties.

CHAPTER 6

FURNITURE

Church offices are probably the most stark working environment to be found. They tend to contain only the bare necessities—a desk (or table) and a chair or two. Frequently the lighting is nearly adequate. Curtains or drapes are neutral colored, and the walls are without pictures. The floor may be bare or covered with linoleum. If carpeted, the carpet tends to be worn and neutral.

This description is not meant to make the typical church office seem depressing, but to suggest an attempt at being utilitarian. Churches regard their offices as work places that do not need decorations and up-to-date furnishings. This attitude may be based on a conviction that money spent on the office can't do the work of the church for people.

Church secretaries know that the surroundings in which a person works affect the kind and amount of work done in a set number of hours. A warm, inviting office encourages work. A stark, cold office suggests one should leave it rather than work.

This contrast between warm and cold offices is not the only one an individual sees in churches. Some church offices have attractive walls and floors, but the office furnishings appear to be discards picked up at local garage sales. Other churches have the latest-style furniture but put it in offices with dismal walls and worn floors. These churches are telling secretaries and visitors about their concept of ministry. Neither gives a good message.

A church office ought to be designed for work, privacy, and sociability. It needs to have a distinctive and inviting aura about it. Although the church is a public place and functions as other institutions such as schools or public buildings, it needs to cultivate its own character.

A church building is an expression of the nature of a particular group of people. Therefore the building should reflect that group's ideas about its Christian purpose and ministry. Church buildings do not have to be painted in monotones like some school buildings. Rather, each part of a church building should be decorated for a specific task. The office is one part with a unique task.

The decor, size, and traffic patterns of an office determine the size of its furniture, where the furniture may be placed, and how much furniture may be used. Most secretaries inherit the amount, size, and location of furniture; few of them have the opportunity to build an office to their specifications. This does not mean a secretary can't have any influence on the placement of furniture.

Decor

Church offices should be pleasant and inviting and help a person feel comfortable. Of course, decorating a room isn't automatically going to do all of these things. The people who work in an office have much to do with the feelings and perceptions of visitors. But the decorating scheme, including the furnishings, speaks volumes to visitors and members alike. The surroundings exude a feeling quite apart from those who work in the office.

A doctor's office, for instance, has a medicinal smell about it. It is clean, and there are magazines on a long table in front of several chairs. The message of the office to the first-time visitor is that something medical happens, the doctor is careful about cleanliness, and it's going to be awhile before the doctor will be ready to see me. These impressions precede any conversation with the nurse or receptionist, who may reinforce or change those initial reactions.

The same sorts of readings occur when someone enters a church office. In this case, the smell might be of mimeograph ink or an odor from the electronic stencil scanning machine. There might be a single chair for a visitor, giving the impression that people aren't considered important since there is only one chair. The visitor comprehends that business, or at least activity by the occupant, is the nature of the room. These impressions may be changed, but they are formed as one enters the office.

Church secretaries must work in church offices. It is up to them to make the office both habitable and inviting. This can be done by repainting walls, adding decorations and plants, and by carefully choosing office furniture. Even though a church office is utilitarian, it can become a nice, comfortable place to work. Above all, the office can be an expression of the church's feeling about its ministry.

Personalizing the Office

A need of every person, church secretaries included, is to make a place one's own. Church secretaries ought to be encouraged to have personal mementoes within the office. It is one means of telling people, "I belong here." This small statement is given through the choice and placement of pictures, plants, paintings, or other decorative items. These can help visitors understand the type of person with whom they are dealing.

Another message a secretary gives by personalizing the office is that the church's ministry is her or his ministry as well. This happens by the manner in which persons are greeted and requests are handled. The personal attitude of the secretary is enhanced by the surroundings.

On the other hand, the secretary must not put too many personal items in an office. Visitors could get the impression that the secretary is trying to take over the church, or members might feel that it is becoming too much the personal domain of one individual. The proper degree of personalization of an office must be learned by trial and error. Each church responds differently to the amount of personalization a secretary may give to an office.

Office Size

The size of an office often depends on which room is next to the pastor's office or study. Except for churches that have carefully considered the type of office they need, the space allocated to an office usually consists of two relatively small rooms. One room is the main office, and the other is called the workroom. The latter contains duplicating machines, supplies, and paper-handling machines in most churches. Its decor is workroom neutral.

The main office may be a bit more spacious than the workroom. It houses the desk, chairs, and, sometimes, file cabinets. This is where the secretary spends most of her or his time.

Quite often a church office is too large or too small, or its layout makes effective work nearly impossible. In these situations, physical changes have to be considered. For instance, the layout of the room may be good except that several usable doors limit wall space. In this setting, placing furniture in an efficient manner becomes a serious problem. The alternative to trying to work in such a limiting space is to close permanently some of the doors in order to increase the amount of office wall space.

Moving walls to increase or decrease office space is a technique used frequently to make offices more functional. The difficulty a church may face is that the office walls may be supporting walls rather than partitions. Moving walls made of plaster is harder and messier than relocating those made with plasterboard or metal. Also, when relocating walls give some thought to major traffic patterns, so the new arrangement of walls does not add many steps a day to the normal routine of an office.

Traffic Patterns

Three types of traffic patterns must be considered when discussing any office, including one in the church. The first pattern is external to the office and relates to the normal way of getting to it (to be discussed in chapter 7). The second and third patterns occur within the office. The second is the manner in which internal movement takes place within the office, i.e., the workers' pattern. The third pattern is that followed by people who go through the main office to get to the pastor's office or study.

The internal office traffic pattern relates to the ease the secretary has in getting from one work place to another. For example, moving from the desk to the file to the desk is a traffic pattern. Moving from the desk to the duplicating room or area and back to the desk is another traffic pattern. Getting to the supply room or cabinet from the desk or duplicating room is another traffic pattern. Any type of trip from one place to another within the office constitutes a traffic pattern.

The objective of a good internal traffic pattern is for the secretary to have an unobstructed path between work areas. For instance, the secretary should not have to go around a desk and a chair to get to a file cabinet if that cabinet is used often. Neither should there be obstacles between any other frequently used work area and the secretary. On the other hand, a doorway isn't considered to be an obstacle. In fact, going from room to room may assist movement, especially when the other room contains duplicating or paper handling equipment or is a storage area. Getting to the door easily is important, however.

One of the reasons for free and easy access to work areas is to cut down on the number of unnecessary trips each day. Safety is another reason for not being forced to go around things. The secretary, in an emergency, must be able to get out of the office quickly. While the probability of an accident in a church office may not be great, the possibility of injury is a condition of humans.

Basic Furniture Needs

The considerations discussed above—the personalization of an office, its decor, its size, and traffic patterns—affect the kinds of furniture that can be put in the office. It is important, for example, to consider the effect on visitors of the number, kinds, and condition of office furniture. In a church, the efficiency of a secretary's work area is not the sole consideration for purchasing and arranging furniture. Since the office is a focal point for church members and leaders, it should be both functional and pleasing.

Office furniture ought to be kept clean and in good repair.

Furniture should be comfortable. There should be enough chairs for two to four visitors in the office. Lighting has to be good enough for an individual to read fine print and to work effectively. Furniture must be arranged so that it is functional without causing a clutter. Equipment should have furniture strong enough to hold it and, if appropriate, large enough to store it.

1. Desks and Chairs

A secretary's desk should have a good surface area for working. A secretary who is given a tiny desk ought not to be expected to accomplish office work effectively. In addition to being large enough, the desk has to be functional, i.e., it needs to have drawers on both sides in which to store supplies and hold files. As a security precaution, there should be a lock on the desk or at least on one set of drawers.

A table or desk extension that holds and stores a typewriter will be needed and is usually placed next to the desk. Sometimes a portable typewriter stand is used in lieu of a pull-out shelf on a desk or a table-like desk extension. Such a stand is convenient when there is sufficient room for it, if the floor covering makes moving it easy, and if there is an electrical outlet near the desk.

Correspondence trays or holders can be placed on one corner of the desk or on a table or file cabinet near the desk. There should be at least four trays for correspondence. They would hold: (1) materials that are just coming into the office, (2) items that have been acted on and need filing, (3) those which are to be acted on by someone else, primarily the pastor, and (4) miscellaneous materials about which there is some question. These holders can be supplemented in larger offices by pigeonhole shelves in which correspondence and other materials can be placed for each staff member as well as volunteer leaders.

An office with a computer will need a separate desk for it. This desk should be specially designed to provide a place for a computer, monitor, disk drives, and probably a printer. (If the printer is large it will need its own stand.) The computer desk should be equipped with an electrical outlet board that can accommodate the computer and its related equipment.

In many church offices, a desk in addition to the secretary's is needed. This desk, usually equipped with a typewriter, is for volunteer workers. It is helpful if the desk has a typewriter storage shelf that allows a person to swing the typewriter out when needed. This storage option makes it possible for the desk's surface to be used for tasks other than typing (such as folding, collating, or bookkeeping).

Each desk will need a chair. The chair should be comfortable and supportive. While there are so-called secretary's chairs, these may not be the best type for a church secretary. A church secretary does more than sit before a typewriter. The chair ought to be comfortable enough to help a secretary relax but be supportive enough for typing. It should be movable.

In addition to secretarial chairs, at least one and possibly three other chairs ought to be in the office. These can be used by service or sales people as well as by visitors to the office. Such chairs can be comfortable, but they must be serviceable and sturdy. There may be a table for magazines and literature, but this isn't necessary or feasible in many church offices.

2. *Furniture for Equipment*

Congregations often place duplicating and paper-handling equipment on top of built-in cabinets in which supplies and materials are stored. While this arrangement saves space, it may not be convenient or conducive to good work. For instance, the counter top may be too high for many secretaries. It is much better to have duplicating equipment on a table or stand that can be moved. However, the machine operator needs easy access to supplies.

Putting equipment on a stand with wheels permits a secretary to move it when there is a problem with light or space. For example, it may be important in some settings to move the stand to another room. Using a movable stand for equipment is useful, although moving a copy machine may be a chore.

No matter the type of furniture used for holding equipment, the stand, table, or counter top has to be sturdy. Most pieces of equipment need strong support. Added to its weight, for example, are the paper and ink or solution for a duplicating machine. A paper-handling machine may be light, but it gains weight when being used.

In addition to the weight of equipment is the vibration created by any machine when it is in operation. Every mechanical device develops a rhythm as it functions. The continued use of a machine can cause a table or stand to become rickety and unsafe. It is not wise for a secretary to keep on operating a piece of equipment when the furniture on which it is placed shows signs of stress.

Another requisite for furniture-holding equipment is a covering under the machine that will withstand the chemicals that are necessary for its use or cleaning. A mimeograph machine should be on a surface that will not be affected by inks or oil or chemicals used to operate and clean it. A postage meter should be on a surface that will not be affected by a water or ink spill. The kind of equipment used will determine the furniture's surface. No matter what it is, the furniture should not be stained or marred by placing and using the machine on it.

Furniture on which equipment is placed has to be movable to permit regular cleaning. Small particles get into the moving parts of machines and cause damage. The best way to prevent unnecessary repair bills is to keep the equipment and the furniture clean. This is done best by regularly cleaning all sides of the stand, table, or counter as well as the machine. Having equipment on mobile stands helps in this cleaning process.

Security often demands that equipment be attached to the furniture on which it is placed. Typewriters are screwed to desk tops, computers are rigged with holding devices, and duplicating machines are anchored to furniture. When this type of security is necessary, portable stands for equipment are not recommended. Equipment should be placed on tables or stands that are attached to the floor or are difficult and awkward to move.

Office machines usually have covers to keep out dust and dirt when they are not in use. Plastic covers are used for most electric and electronic products; therefore, the furniture on which they are placed is not affected by additional weight from such covers. A noise-proofing cover for a typewriter or printer, however, can add significantly to the weight of the machine. The stand or table on which it is located must be able to hold the additional weight while the machine is running.

It is a good idea for most pieces of equipment to be stored within furniture rather than on top when not in use. This suggests that furniture for most small machines have shelves or an enclosure in which the machines can be placed and from which they can be retrieved easily. It may mean that some equipment is placed on mobile furniture so it can be wheeled into locked closets or rooms when it isn't being used.

3. *Files, Bookcases, Cabinets, and Shelves*

The key criterion for these types of furniture is durability. Unless there are special reasons for not having metal in an office, file cabinets, storage cabinets, and shelves need to be made of strong metal. In most offices, metal bookcases are more functional than wooden ones.

Metal shelves and files are not only more durable, they are easier to clean, repair, and paint than wooden items. These attributes can make redecorating and maintenance much easier than when wooden furniture is involved. In addition, metal items are, by nature, not usually built into office walls. This means they are movable without the work commonly associated with having to take out built-in bookcases, for example.

Shelves and storage cabinets tend to be in storerooms. This furniture needs to be sturdy, accessible, resistant to water, mildew, rust, and fire, and it should be easily cleaned. When important documents are stored in church files, the file cabinet ought to be fire resistant. Since the number of such documents is small for any particular church, the fire-resistant cabinet needn't be large. No matter how small it is, however, such a file cabinet will be relatively expensive.

A failing of many churches is that they continue to add storage capacity and fail to discard unneeded materials or files. It is easier to get a new file cabinet than it is to go through an existing one and discard unimportant items. That's the reason a secretary should limit the number of file cabinets needed for storage and for current files. The secretary will force herself or himself to do a weeding out on at least an annual basis.

Cabinets used for storing supplies should have doors that lock. Paper, pencils, paper clips, rubber bands, and staples have a way of disappearing rapidly. A door with a lock on it—if the lock is used—tends to discourage permanent borrowing of small office supplies. Unless the cabinet is locked, however, people will not be discouraged from taking these supplies.

Cardboard boxes or files placed on metal shelves are adequate for most stored documents. It isn't necessary to purchase file cabinets to store unused or historical documents. Most of them can be kept in a room on metal shelving. Of course, the room will need to have ventilation and humidity control.

Bookcases for the office should be limited in number and size. They will contain items necessary for the operation of equipment, descriptive documents relating to the church and its programs, and books important to the functions of a secretary such as a telephone directory and a dictionary. Large bookcases are inappropriate in a church office. Such bookcases are needed in the pastor's office and in the church library, and that is where they should be kept.

4. Lights

A church office needs excellent lighting. Lighting depends not only on the wattage of bulbs but also on the number and location of fixtures. Adequate office lighting includes one or more overhead lights (depending on the size of the room and the fixture—a large flourescent fixture is preferable), and a lamp for each desk, typing area, and work area.

It is important to have a working light fixture near each machine to ensure safety and facilitate output. For machines on movable stands, one or two stationary lamps may be adequate so long as the equipment can be brought to the light fixtures.

A desk lamp should not be decorative only. It needs to be utilitarian as well. A lamp may be attached to the desk (clamped on the edge of the desk top), but it needs to be of an extension-neck variety so it can be adjusted and directed to work areas. It is very important to illuminate adequately materials that are being typed or put into computers, or figures that are being added or recorded.

If an office errs in lighting it should be in having too many lamps and too much light. Lights can be turned off when they are not needed. On the other hand, a secretary should not tolerate inadequate lighting.

Using extension cords to add lighting fixtures to an office or having multiple plugs in one outlet may be dangerous. Calling an electrician, talking with the custodian, or questioning an office-machine dealer will help a secretary recognize what might be a questionable practice for hooking up lights and electrical machines.

An electrical wire or an extension cord should not be run under a carpet or routed through a traffic pattern or laid where it interferes with the movement of chairs or office stands. Repeatedly stepping on a cord or rolling a chair or machine over it could break it or wear off its insulating cover. Also, a bump in the carpet may cause a person to stumble or a chair or machine to tip over. These incidents can create fires and cause preventable accidents.

5. *Coat Racks and Wastebaskets*

Two other types of basic furnishings in a church office are a rack on which coats and sweaters may be hung and receptacles for waste paper. These items, sometimes regarded as too mundane to think about, are essential pieces of furniture in every office. They are small enough to be screened from view, or they can be a part of the normal decor of the office. Their placement should be unobtrusive so as not to interfere with any traffic pattern.

A coat rack may be attached to a wall in a storeroom. It is out of the way and not noticeable. A free-standing rack may be in the hallway outside the door of the main office. Generally, a coat rack should not be in the main office because it uses work space. However, some church offices have a built-in closet for coats and robes. The closet may be used also for storing supplies or office devices such as stepping stools or small step ladders. If there is a closet, it should be used for the coats and wraps of secretaries and guests.

Every office needs more than one wastebasket. One wastebasket will be near the secretary's desk. This may be small and can fit in with the office decor. At least one wastebasket or bin should be in the workroom. This container needs to be large and functional. It will be used for discarded stencils, empty ink cans or bottles, and cleanups from messes of one sort or another. Large plastic containers are useful for this function, as are large metal waste containers with plastic liners. The wastebaskets ought not to be too large for easy handling or too heavy to empty when they are full.

Special Jobs or Needs

Church offices deal with people with special needs such as older persons and handicapped individuals. In each case, the furniture in the office needs to be suited to them. This may mean purchasing chairs that are more comfortable, desks or tables that can be accommodated to volunteers or employees who are confined to wheelchairs, arranging traffic patterns to make them wider and more direct, and installing special lighting in work areas for those who have difficulty seeing. Caring for these needs may take a few extra dollars, but the result will be a wider opportunity for different kinds of workers and more productive and satisfied office staff.

A different kind of need arises when the office is shared or is a part of a large room the other section of which is used for meetings. In this kind of situation, a conference table will probably occupy part of the room. Sharing a work area is not an ideal setting. However, it can be handled by installing room dividers which may be heavy commercial plastic divider curtains, folding doors, or a more modest screen-type barrier.

Another approach to the effective use of a shared office is to schedule one's work around the use of the room for meetings. This will require cooperation among the secretary and those who use the room for meetings. The secretary could do office work when there is no meeting, and workroom activity when meetings are being held. This separation of tasks won't be possible at all times, but it can take care of most interruptions.

In churches with volunteers who use the telephone a great deal, a special room may be needed for their work. Separating their telephone work from their "silent" activities, like typing, transcribing dictation, or record keeping, can relieve potential frustration. The telephone room will need to be kept locked and should be opened by the secretary only for authorized persons. Of course, it will contain a separate telephone or two as decided by the program committee of the church.

Carpets and Couches

A carpet is a sound-deadening, draft-reducing investment for an office. An office carpet should be of commercial grade, but it ought to be an integral part of a pleasing decor. It doesn't have to be drab to be durable and stain resistant. Office carpets should be replaced every five to seven years.

Two areas of a carpet need special protection in an office. The first of these is the entrance way. A throw rug outside the door or a plastic runner extending part of the way into the office is an excellent investment. The runner keeps the carpet clean. A throw rug or a small mat may be put outside the office door as an alternative to a plastic runner in the office. No matter which protective device is used—a plastic runner, a mat, or a throw rug—it should not be loose or placed in such a way that it can cause a person to trip or fall. This precaution is particularly important when older persons regularly use the office.

The second area needing protective cover is under the secretary's chair. Plastic sheets for this purpose are available from any office-supply dealer. An office should invest in one such mat for the secretary's chair and for work areas elsewhere.

Another considerate purchase is a cushioned mat for work areas which require standing. For instance, a cushioned mat would be useful when the secretary is using the duplicating machine. This mat would be on top of a protective plastic sheet even if the floor is not carpeted.

A couch in an office saves space when compared to two or three chairs. The basic consideration in deciding whether to use a couch is the wall space and office arrangement. It may not be possible to put a couch in the office and retain good traffic patterns. In this case, use chairs. The couch has the same function but tends to be more functional than chairs.

Amenities

Offices may contain, in addition to basic furniture, literature racks, tables for materials to read or take, holders for wet items such as umbrellas and boots, and heaters. These can be added where they are needed and space is available.

No piece of furniture that doesn't have a utilitarian function should be in a church office. However, small items that enhance the office decor can be considered utilitarian so long as the office isn't cluttered or traffic patterns interrupted.

Other items such as ash trays may be limited by the policies and teachings of the church or the desires of the secretary. Included in this category are small pieces of wrapped candy or mints. These little amenities can add to the warmth of the church office.

CHAPTER 7

OFFICE LOCATION

As previous discussions have shown, an office is the nerve center of a church. It is where administrative and program work is done. It is where records are stored and maintained. It is where people call for information or help. It is where vendors come to sell office materials, equipment, and supplies.

The church office is not the pastor's study. The study is where the pastor studies, counsels, or otherwise works. The distinction between the church office and the pastor's study is lost by congregations that think a church office is unnecessary because they don't have a secretary. Every church needs an office in which someone does administrative work. The pastor may do some administration, but that is not her or his primary role. Being a secretary, and being in charge of the church office, is the ministry of a person other than the pastor.

The pastor often selects the location of the church office in spite of not being in charge of it. This is because the location of the church office is based pretty much on where the pastor's study is located. When the pastor chooses the study site, the church office tends to be close by. Proximity to the church office is critical for most pastors.

However, being close to the church office is not necessary or even desirable for a few pastors. That's one reason for changing the location of the church office. For example, a pastor who has a particular emphasis in ministry, such as the extensive use of media, may feel justified in shifting the office's location so the comings and goings there do not disturb her or him. Another pastor may change the office location because he or she feels it is not convenient enough for people to find. Or a pastor may feel it is too close to the study for those who come for counseling to maintain their anonymity.

Regardless of the reason for shifting the church office's location, any change will require a certain amount of electrical rewiring as well as relocating of telephone lines. Shifting an office location can be expensive. It is up to the secretary to assist the pastor in thinking through the change carefully before it is done.

Considerations for an Office in the Church

The location of the church office greatly affects its potential for ministry because location may determine accessibility, size, and the degree of privacy the office affords when an individual has a confidential discussion with the pastor. Location also affects security and other working conditions of the secretary.

1. Accessibility

The church office is the first continuing link an individual has with the church. The contact may come through a telephone call for information or a casual drop-in visit for information about the church. The record of the call or visit is kept in the office and shared with the pastor (regardless of the church's size). After that, the internal workings of the church's ministry are activated toward the visitor. But the potential for ministry has already been decided by the visitor. This decision is based, in part, on how easy it was to get to the office for the information he or she needed.

Access to a church's office is as important as its decor and the demeanor of its occupants. Therefore, the office ought to be located in a room or rooms that are evident and logical to anyone who casually visits a church. It should be close to an outside entrance. (This entrance probably will be different from the sanctuary entrance.)

Locating the office so that it has to be reached by following a little used outside path, such as an overgrown brick walk, is an invitation to people not to come. An office door located on the rear or side of the building will not be helpful to the church. When visitors or members must go around the building or can't find the office easily, they will give up looking. This results in disenchantment on their part and a lost opportunity for ministry by the church.

Clearly evident outside signs pointing to the church office help people find it easily. These signs should be visible from the street. The entrance should be lighted and marked. If the door is kept locked, a working bell is a necessity. A speaker near the door can be useful when the church office is down a hallway from the outside entrance.

It is important to have signs inside the main entrance to the building pointing to the office. People can get lost and become frightened in a seemingly empty building. These signs should be in all hallways. If some members object to such signs, remind them that it is in the church's best interests to help people locate the office, especially in an emergency.

It is helpful not only to visitors but to secretaries as well if the office is not placed in a remote part of the building. Easy access to the outside and visibility from a street make the office safer for employees and volunteers. It makes little sense, for example, to have to go through the sanctuary to get to the office. This is an unnecessary barrier to the outside world.

The church's office should be on ground level if possible. If this is not practical, it ought to be on the same level as the main entrance rather than a flight of stairs up or down. Putting the office on the same level as the main entrance enables people who have difficulty with stairs to get to it readily once they enter the building. An exterior ramp with a railing leading to the office door is helpful to older persons and the disabled. When one has to climb stairs or ride an elevator to the office, simply getting there may discourage the individual.

The outside door to the office should be easy to open. Small children, the elderly, and individuals with physical disabilities shouldn't have to ask for assistance to open the office door. The size and condition of the door are considerations in its ease of operation.

As a matter of energy savings as well as safety, the office should be protected from the exterior of the building by a hallway or vestibule. This entrance way can be used for coat racks and mats to wipe shoes and boots, and provides a chance for people to recover from the weather. A glass entrance into the office is used in some churches to allow secretaries to observe people before they enter the office. This may not be practical in certain kinds of church settings.

2. *Size*

Another consideration in location is the size of the office. An office should be of sufficient size to allow a secretary to work comfortably and efficiently. The office should not be packed full of furniture, files, and equipment. It needs to have space for visitors, service people, and the workers.

Additional rooms near the office may be needed for work and storage. In fact, the workroom and storeroom may be one and the same. A closet or a cabinet in a workroom might be the storage area for a church. Regardless of the actual arrangement, these areas have to be large enough for the secretary or a volunteer to operate equipment safely and to get supplies in and out. It is useless to have paper-handling equipment if there is no room for a table on which it can be used.

As has been indicated before, the work and storage areas should be separated from that part of the office reserved for the normal routine of greeting visitors, handling correspondence, and receiving individuals waiting to see the pastor. When there isn't a separate room, the use of files or other screening devices can make work areas distinct.

3. *Confidentiality*

It is important for church offices located next to a pastor's study to have an extra sound-deadening barrier, such as bookcases, wall hangings, files, or cabinets, on the common wall with the study. This will cut down two-way interference and make it easier for a pastor to have confidential counseling sessions.

Another method of ensuring confidentiality is to install a second entrance to the pastor's study other than through the church office. This is particularly important for some people with whom the pastor counsels. The second entrance might have its own exterior exit, and the waiting area might be a hallway with a few chairs. A sensitive secretary can make this an attractive place for persons waiting to see the pastor.

4. *Security*

The office should be lockable. A church invests quite a lot of money in its office equipment and furniture, and it has historical and confidential files. These need protection. Also, the church office has to be located in a part of the building that ensures security for workers during their day or evening routine and when no one else is in the office.

Security alarms hooked up with the police department are a useful adjunct to other precautions. However, security devices are not helpful if the door can't be locked. By the time a police officer gets to the building, much damage can be done. The church office needs to be in a part of the building that gives it protection, and it needs a door that can be locked.

5. *Privacy*

A church secretary needs a private place to go to get away from the office. This place has to be close by because the secretary must listen for telephone calls and watch for visitors. The private place shouldn't be in a storeroom or work area but might be in a lounge or similar setting. Having a separate room may be impractical in a few churches, but consideration of a secretary's needs demands that a church provide such a space near or in the office.

These five needs of a good office location may determine whether a church puts its office in the pastor's home or in the church building or both.

Office in the Parsonage

The previous discussion has assumed that the church office will be in the church building. This may be an invalid assumption, especially for small congregations. However, a church office will have the same requirements whether it is located in the church building or in a parsonage.

Historically, Protestant churches have assumed that the pastor's residence, the parsonage, was a public place. It has been used as the home for the pastor and her or his family, but the assumption has been that its rooms were available for meetings and for the church's office. While these sentiments may continue in some places, it currently is assumed rather widely that the primary function of the parsonage is to be the home of the pastor.

Even so, church offices are sometimes still kept in parsonages. Usually the office is in a room that is separated from or can be locked off from other parts of the house. The office usually has an outside entrance of its own, so that people don't have to go through the parsonage to get to it. It may or may not contain duplicating and paper-handling equipment, but it generally contains a cabinet or a closet for storing supplies. Files, especially current ones, are in at least one cabinet.

Churches using a parsonage for handling their office needs have assumed the pastor would perform most of the administrative details including typing, duplicating, and keeping records. That assumption is no longer valid. Pastors, rightfully, are asking volunteers and secretaries to handle those tasks. This leads to the complication of having an outsider come into the parsonage to work in the church's office.

A church office located in a parsonage should observe the requirements of accessibility, size, confidentiality, security, and privacy previously discussed. The only difference is the building where the office is located.

In instances where the parsonage contains the church

office, the parsonage is usually next door to the church. If it isn't, a sign on the main entrance of the church building should tell visitors where the office is (street address plus minimal directions) and give the telephone number. A church should not frustrate its visitors or members by giving inadequate or inaccurate information on directional signs.

It is especially important, when the church's office is in the parsonage, to remember the distinction between the pastor's study and the church office. A pastor may choose to have a study in the parsonage. The church should not assume the study takes the place of an office. While in smaller congregations some office duties may be performed by the pastor, it is important for a church to provide an office and a secretary. A secretary should not be cheated out of her or his ministry because of an overly ambitious pastor or niggardly congregation.

The telephone may pose a problem when the church office is in the parsonage. The office should have a separate line. It isn't fair to the pastor's family not to have their own telephone service. Different telephone numbers for home and office allow people to call the office without bothering the parsonage family. A separate telephone gives the pastor's family the privacy it needs.

Cleaning and decorating the office when it is in the parsonage is the responsibility of the church, not of the parsonage family. A church's office, no matter where it is located, should be kept clean, painted, and furnished by the custodian. Responsibility for seeing that these jobs are taken care of regularly rests with the administrative committee of the church.

A secretary who works in the church office in the parsonage should be treated as though he or she is working in the church building. It is not appropriate to treat the secretary as a guest. Such a secretary is not a guest; it just happens that the place of work is in a home. This means that if there is to be coffee in the office, the church should purchase a coffee maker and install a sink where it can be cleaned. The secretary should not have to depend on or bother the parsonage family to make coffee.

The entire operation of a church office should be in one place. For example, a secretary who works in a parsonage office shouldn't be expected to run to the church building to do half of the work such as duplicating. This kind of split office might occasion several trips each work day. If there is room at the church for such things, a church office probably could be built there as well. If it's a matter of heating or cooling the office, these can be accomplished by mobile units.

Multiple Offices

Occasionally, churches need more than a single office. This may be owing to the size of the congregation or it may be the result of different types of ministries. Often in these situations, each office has a distinct function. If this is not the case, it is up to the secretaries to rethink the functions of the total office and assign them to separate offices.

For instance, one office might be devoted to administrative detail, such as finances and record keeping. Maintaining pledge receipts, balancing checkbooks, keeping membership records, and handling correspondence related to these matters might be the responsibility of that office. Another office might handle correspondence, appointments, and scheduling of building use. Whatever the distinction, each office needs to have specific and not overlapping tasks.

A multiple-office church usually has one office related to

the senior pastor and one secretary for each additional staff member. In this setting, there generally is an office manager whose tasks include personnel matters and general oversight of the various secretaries. When no office manager is designated, the duties of administering the offices rest on the secretary of the senior pastor. However, multiple-office churches should appoint an administrator of the offices.

Ordering supplies, purchasing equipment, and keeping the equipment maintained are of critical importance in multiple-office churches. These tasks need to be centralized in order to save money and effort. Centralization usually occurs when the authority to be an administrator is designated by the senior pastor or by the administrative committee overseeing the offices.

Regardless of the internal administrative workings of the offices, the location of the main office should be near a major traffic pattern into the building and an important internal traffic pattern. In this sense, it should be at a crossroads so it is easy to find and readily apparent. Other offices should be marked clearly, and a central direction board should be placed by the main office entrance.

A common workroom can accommodate several offices. This room probably will have one staff person who is responsible for the supplies and equipment in it. The work area in multiple-office churches will not include the storage area for files and records. These will be in a separate room.

In multiple-office churches, each office will need to have its own file cabinets and small storage areas. These will enable secretaries to keep tabs on their own work spheres and save time that would be used in going to a central storage and supply room. Of course, the secretaries will be required to submit inventories and supply needs to the central supply room monthly. The secretaries will utilize the central storage room for noncurrent files and records.

Security for each office will be handled by the main office. Keys and an alarm system will be administered through a master control in the central office. In order to manage office security adequately, all offices should be relatively close together. This could mean they are on the same hallway near the main office. None should be in an obscure part of the building, although, for programmatic purposes, one office may be in a particular section of the building.

Each office should be of a size adequate for its needs. None should be too small to accommodate a secretary, although the work area doesn't have to be as large as is necessary for single-office churches. In some settings, an office in a multiple-office church could be just large enough to hold a small desk and telephone.

Each office should meet the requirements of accessibility and confidentiality outlined previously. A common lounge can be used as a private place for secretaries. The lounge could have facilities, such as a microwave and a sink, that secretaries might use for preparing lunches. Also, a check-in system for secretaries should be enforced, not so much to keep time records as to assure safety. Multiple-office churches are responsible for each of their secretaries, including their security, while they are on the job.

CHAPTER 8

OFFICE HOURS

"When do you open?" is a query secretaries hear often. Volunteers and church leaders who need to have the office provide information or services know they have to get there when the secretary can help them. Also, they are used to dealing with offices that open and close at particular times. They need to know the schedule so as not to waste their time.

On the other hand, people are aware that pastors may or may not function according to the same timetable as the church office. The pastor's schedule doesn't have to be the same as that of the church office. A general perception is that it shouldn't. The pastor ought to be doing things other than staying in the office. In addition, the pastor is not required to be in the church when the office is open.

Set Office Hours

Church offices need to operate on scheduled hours. The schedule, specifying the days and hours the office is open, not only alerts the secretary to when he or she should be on duty but it tells the public when the office can be expected to be open. Thus people know when their calls might be answered or their visits might produce results. The office schedule, while it is not a guarantee, does indicate when an individual might make an appointment with or send a message to the pastor.

People need regularly scheduled office hours because they function on the basis of habits and routines. Once a schedule is set, even though they might not like it, it provides structure. A secretary also needs to have the schedule so that he or she will be able to plan work and personal activities. Working on a helter-skelter basis is not conducive to enriching family life, for example.

The primary question a church must answer, when deciding on an office schedule, is, "What office hours will be best for our ministry?" There is no easy answer to the question. For example, with an increasing number of women working outside the home, it becomes more and more difficult to contact them or for them to contact the church during the day. This would suggest that office hours between five and eight o'clock in the evening might be convenient for this group.

Retired persons from age fifty-five onward may prefer to be involved with the church during the daylight hours. This may mean the church office should be open from ten o'clock in the morning until about four in the afternoon. This schedule would be most convenient for the retired individuals in the parish.

Persons who have rotating work shifts in stores, factories, or service occupations could be accommodated best if the church office stayed open at least twelve hours a day. This would given them a chance to get to the office before or after work regardless of their shift.

Parishoners who travel or who work two jobs during the week would be benefited by church office hours on Saturday and possibly following worship service on Sunday. In some churches, Sunday evening might be a good time for the office to be open for business.

In certain kinds of ministries, such as suicide prevention,

lost children hotlines, family abuse, rape, and the like, people need twenty-four-hour access to a church office. In these cases, the need is for someone to answer a telephone, not for an office to go to. Yet, a drop-in location may be necessary for some people touched by special ministries. In churches sponsoring such ministries, the church office might never be closed in a technical sense. However, secretaries would be present for a part of every day to take care of records, references to other agencies, and follow-ups promised by the program person.

A church must decide whom it is going to serve before it establishes office hours. When a schedule is drawn up, it will eliminate some people's chances of getting into the office or calling it at times convenient to them. Unfortunately, the question "Who is to be served by our ministry?" is not considered by most congregations in setting office hours. Churches create office hours that coincide with the business hours that are customary in the community. For instance, if most stores in the community are open from 8:00 A.M. until 5:00 A.M., the church feels its office ought to be open then as well.

A secretary who is interested in making the most of her or his ministry will help a church consider the consequences of various types of scheduled office hours. The assumption that the church should be open when every other business is open should be discouraged. It is wise and appropriate for a secretary to list options of times when he or she might be willing to work that are different from the hours kept by other community businesses. These options could include one or two evenings a week and a Saturday morning.

A secretary may, as another option, test different schedules for two or three months at a time. If he or she keeps track of calls, visits, and work accomplishments for each period, comparisons between the schedules can help an administrative committee develop an office schedule to better serve the needs of members, visitors, and secretaries.

Previous discussions have suggested that split hours for church offices may be good for some congregations. This would mean afternoon and evening or morning and evening hours. Splitting times may provide better service in some communities. Relying exclusively on evening hours can be best for other churches. The issue surrounding office hours is not whether there needs to be a schedule but that the nature of the schedule should be to enhance the church's ministry.

A decision about an office hour schedule is not final and forever. A change in the focus of ministry in a church may demand a new office schedule. However, schedules should be changed only when there is a sufficient reason for adjustment. Whims or personal tinkering with office hours without cause is not justifiable. A secretary can help a congregation be reasonable in making adjustments in the office schedule. However, any adjustments will require a secretary to be flexible in her or his demands about working time.

When it is impossible to maintain scheduled office hours because of a secretary's illness or vacation, and a replacement cannot be found or isn't desired, an electronic answering machine is an option. The investment in such a machine pays for itself in a short time. A secretary or volunteer can go to the office or use a remote device to get a playback of messages any time during the day or evening. Then the task is to route the messages to the proper persons and make return calls as needed. The use of this procedure is widespread, and even those who dislike talking to a machine understand that the secretary is not always able to be in the office.

A telephone answering machine may be helpful for any church that wants to cover the office during hours when it is closed. An option for these congregations is to give a number during the answering message that people can call in an emergency. If this is done, the number that is given should be attended so that emergencies can be dealt with. For example, a person who calls the emergency number should be able to get in touch with an individual, not another answering machine. If several people agree to respond to emergencies, the contact number given in the recorded message on the machine will need to be changed each time a different person is on call.

Let People Know

A requirement for any office is to advertise the hours when it is open. It doesn't make sense to shift the office hours to accommodate a particular group in the community and not let those people know about the change. For example, a church may decide to create new office hours for Tuesday and Wednesday evenings and Saturday morning in order to better meet the needs of those who work during the day. If that schedule is posted only on the inside of an office door, it probably will be ineffective because it won't reach those to whom it is aimed.

Schedules have to be advertised. They should be posted on the office door, the exterior door, and announced in publications of the church. In many communities, church advertisements in the yellow pages could include office hours for no additional cost. Also, newspaper ads giving the hours of worship could include the church's office hours. Publishing office hours is an invitation and a welcome to different groups in the church and in the community.

When a change in hours is anticipated, people ought to be informed of the shift two or three weeks in advance. Special ads will be needed to alert them to the impending change.

Even so, some people will miss the announcements and become disturbed when they cannot get into the office according to their old habits. In order to relieve such frustration, the new schedule should be posted on the outside of the office door, along with the effective date of change, several weeks after the new hours are in effect.

Keeping Hours—but Flexibly

A secretary is hired for a certain number of hours of work each day. On most days, it is possible to leave within a few minutes of quitting time. There are days, however, when an extra quarter hour or half hour is necessary either to finish a job or to accommodate someone's request for assistance.

A secretary who wants to quit precisely on time should begin on schedule, not waste one minute during the day, and not dawdle over lunch or linger at breaks. Since secretaries are human, these stipulations are bent on many days. For example, at least once in a while the secretary will be late (because of the weather, the car, the traffic, a sick spouse or child), and occasionally she or he will find breaks and lunch more enjoyable than working. It is worthwhile to remember these few minutes snatched here and there when the job at hand requires a few minutes extra at the end of a day.

This doesn't mean a secretary should be willing to extend the workday for any and every request. A pastor who procrastinates often and doesn't get work to the secretary until late in the day doesn't deserve extra time from the secretary. Therefore, unless the work is of an emergency nature, it should be held over until the next day. A pastor who puts things off shouldn't be allowed to make a secretary regularly stay beyond quitting time.

Being flexible with office-hour schedules means that the secretary may come in an hour late once a month because the pastor is counseling a person and wants the secretary in the office during the session. This is a special arrangement, and it can be set up in advance. On the other hand, an emergency situation, an accident, or a sudden illness involving a church member, may prompt the pastor to ask the secretary to be the contact person in the office while he or she goes to the hospital. Covering the office in such a situation may extend beyond quitting time.

A church's ministry never fits neatly into regularly scheduled office hours. On the average, however, a secretary can adjust her or his life to the demands of the office schedule. A person in ministry should realize that occasionally he or she will be asked to make adjustments in his or her personal schedule.

Special Arrangements

There are times when a secretary must make special arrangements for working. New arrangements become necessary if the church building is being renovated or has been destroyed or severely damaged. New office schedules will be needed. The new office hours will depend on where the temporary church office is located, which in turn will depend on where the work can be done.

Often another church will encourage a congregation to use part of its facilities temporarily. When this happens, the secretary is set up in a temporary office, which is usually no office at all. In addition, the normal office schedule is abandoned and a new one established, based on what hours are possible in the new location.

The catch in such arrangements is that these conditions might last for a year to a year and a half. This is a long time to abide in temporary quarters. However, at some time during this period, the pastor and secretary can find more suitable quarters and establish a schedule more appropriate to the conditions of the new place.

Another situation calling for special arrangements is when something happens to the pastor. Usually this is an accident or a health problem. The secretary's load becomes greater, at least temporarily, because he or she must follow through on more items than when the pastor is at the church. This extra work might require more time out of the office and entail keeping some appointments that can't be accommodated during the work day. The word "temporary" is used loosely for these situations. Disability tends to linger.

Another situation demanding special arrangements is when the pastor leaves and is not replaced immediately. An interim pastor might be filling in during a search process, but the work of the secretary can alter considerably. When the work load is changed because of a pastoral vacancy, office hours might need to be shifted or extended.

A primary consideration for the secretary in making special arrangements is discovering the nature of the tasks he or she is being asked to do. The new tasks might call for being personally bonded, working with legal documents, and assuming authority for administering much of the work of the parish. No matter what the new requirements of the job might be, the secretary has to have, in writing, from the administrative committee of the church, a description of these new duties and the necessary authority to fulfill them.

When such special situations arise, the secretary must

negotiate new office schedules that will allow her or him to do the necessary work without being overloaded. This could mean arranging for temporary assistance in the form of a part-time volunteer or another paid secretary. Another option is to utilize a quick-print business for all the duplicating done previously by the secretary. In either case, budgets have to be redrawn.

CHAPTER 9

CONCLUSION

Secretary is a *position* that's occupied by a *person*. This sequence is important. The position is important to the proper functioning of the church. However, the individual holding the position is a representative and interpreter of the church to the public as well as to church members. The reason for this is that a secretary is the first person a visitor meets when he or she calls or walks into the church office. The call or visit may be a first contact with the church or it may be a routine occurrence. No matter which it is, the secretary's attitude and demeanor speak volumes about the church.

Not everyone can be a church secretary. The pressures, great at times, come from the pastor, the administrative committee to whom the secretary reports, and church members. Each of these persons or groups feels that their needs are special and must be met immediately. Being able to handle such conflicting demands with grace and authority is a task for selected persons. The most dedicated of these people feel being a secretary is an expression of their personal ministry.

A secretary may be full-time, part-time, paid, or volunteer. It makes no difference which of these an individual is, the tasks and responsibilities are the same: handling correspondence, answering the telephone, forwarding messages, keeping records, typing, duplicating, filing, and scheduling. Local needs may expand this list. The specific details under each of these headings are worked out between the secretary and the administrative committee to whom the person reports.

The duties of the secretary are spelled out clearly in the job description, which is agreed upon by the pastor, the administrative committee, and the secretary. Any deviation from the job description may result in a major confrontation. Changes in the description can be worked out at any time, but these should be attached to the original agreement or a new agreement ought to be created and signed.

The secretary is not a personal helper of the pastor. The secretary is hired by the church to help keep the church organization running and to relieve the pastor of some administrative duties. Therefore, doing jobs of a personal nature for the pastor is not required and generally is not appropriate. Such personal jobs include purchasing cards for an anniversary or birthday in the pastor's family, going on errands specifically for the pastor's benefit, and babysitting for the pastor's child. Some secretaries occasionally do a personal chore but it should not become habitual.

Organizing

Two of the themes of this book have been that it is essential for those who are in charge of church offices to plan carefully and to get themselves and the office organized so that work can be done efficiently and well. It is hard to imagine a well run office that is not well organized.

Office organization, as discussed in this book, focuses not just on developing a good filing system and scheduling and calendaring procedures. It includes location of the furniture; the availability of different kinds of equipment to help the secretary and/or volunteers do their jobs effectively and on time; the decor and atmosphere of the office, its location, and the hours when it is open. Each of these specific items has been dealt with in a separate chapter.

Organizing, however, goes further than keeping things in order and making lists. Planning and organizing are ways of life. They are not one-time-a-year events like spring housecleaning. They are habits in practice. Unfortunately, not every church office can boast of an organized life pattern based on planning.

Since an office reflects the work and life-styles of those who are in charge, the secretary and pastor or just the pastor, they must exercise planning and organizing skills and practices. By the same token, it is the responsibility of the secretary and the pastor to create a positive working attitude about the office within the church. This attitude should reflect concern for planning the church's life and organizing it so that members know about its purpose and program, and are continually reminded of its activity schedules.

Purpose

The primary purpose of the church office is to serve its members and the public. How well this is accomplished depends upon the sensitivity of the pastor, the administration committee, and the secretary. Concern for widespread participation in and knowledge about the church will help determine office hours and office location. A church office will seek to be open when people can get to it for things they need. It will be located in an easily accessible and public part of the building.

Another purpose of the office is to maintain the church's organizational life. Keeping accurate records of members, attendance, finances, committee meetings and actions, and handling requests is essential. The volume of such work will vary according to the size and activity level of the church. However, to accomplish this part of the purpose requires attention to detail and overcoming the tendency to procrastinate.

A church office, in spite of being for the members and the public, must function under the leadership of an individual. Of course, this person will operate under the guidelines, policies, and practices approved by an administrative committee. Even so, there will be a boss. That usually is the pastor. The secretary will have responsibilities and will be given freedom to do specified tasks. However, in the long run, the pastor is in charge of the church office.

Some pastors will need little or no direction in handling the office. Other pastors are not interested in administrative work. No matter. The administrative committee will work with the pastor to help establish an orderly and organized environment within which to carry out ministry.

Finally, office procedures are a cooperative venture from beginning to end. They depend on pastor, secretary, other staff members, and church members to observe and follow them. A church must take time to plan and organize its office, but it has to do it in the best interests of those who work there *and* those who use it. When both groups are considered carefully, the organization will be served well.